The Weird Kid's Guide to Particularly Odd Horror and Sci-Fi Movies

Editors: Steven Peros and Mark Bailey
Co-Editor: Steven B. Orkin

Reviews by Mark Bailey, Larry Blamire, Dan Madigan, Tracy Mercer, Steven B. Orkin, Mike Peros, Steven Peros, Nadia Robertson, Brian R. Solomon, and Phoef Sutton

Monster Kid

[mänstər kid] **noun**

a passionate fan of early to mid-twentieth century monster movies, as well as the ~~magazines, toys, model kits, and creature~~ feature television shows they inspired

DEDICATION

Most of the movies profiled in these pages were conceived and created by dream makers in the City of Angels.

This book is dedicated to all those affected by the 2025 wildfires.

Los Angeles will live on, as will the Angelenos who bravely share their beautifully mad dreams.

Cinema Bizarro
©2025 Steven Peros

All rights reserved.

No part of this book may be reproduced in any form or by any means, electronic, mechanical, digital, photocopying, or recording, except for inclusion of a review without permission in writing from the publisher.

Published in the USA by:
BearManor Media
1317 Edgewater Dr. #110
Orlando FL 32804
www.BearManorMedia.com

ISBN-10: 979-8-88771-679-4 Cinema Bizarro
ISBN-13: 979-8-88771-680-0 Cinema Bizarro hb

Art, Design, and Layout: Mark Bailey

TABLE OF CONTENTS

Introduction - Steven Peros 1

The Authors 5

A Note from Mark Bailey 9

A Note from Steven B. Orkin 10

KILLER PLANTS

The Thing from Another World - Dan Madigan 11

Invasion of the Body Snatchers - Tracy Mercer 15

From Hell It Came - Mike Peros 19

The Unknown Terror - Larry Blamire 23

The Woman Eater - Nadia Robertson 27

The Little Shop of Horrors - Phoef Sutton 31

The Day of the Triffids - Nadia Robertson 35

Matango - Brian R. Solomon 39

Die, Monster, Die! - Phoef Sutton 43

Dr. Terror's House of Horrors - Nadia Robertson 47

The Navy vs. the Night Monsters - Tracy Mercer 51

Venus Flytrap - Mark Bailey 55

Maneater of Hydra - Steven B. Orkin 59

Brides of Blood - Tracy Mercer 63

 TOC

ECCENTRIC ALIENS

Robot Monster - Phoef Sutton...67

The Quatermass Xperiment - Steven Peros...71

The Crawling Eye - Mike Peros...75

Warning from Space - Brian R. Solomon..79

Kronos - Nadia Robertson...83

The Monolith Monsters - Phoef Sutton...87

Quatermass 2 - Steven Peros..91

The Blob - Dan Madigan..95

The Brain from Planet Arous - Mike Peros...99

I Married a Monster from Outer Space - Larry Blamire.....................103

Night of the Blood Beast - Larry Blamire..107

Invisible Invaders - Mike Peros...111

The Creeping Terror - Tracy Mercer..115

Dogora - Brian R. Solomon..119

The Bubble - Nadia Robertson..123

The X from Outer Space - Brian R. Solomon......................................127

The Green Slime - Dan Madigan...131

Goke, Body Snatcher from Hell - Brian R. Solomon..........................135

 TOC

THE WEIRD WEST

Weird West Roundup of the 1930s - Larry Blamire 139

Weird West Roundup of the 1940s - Larry Blamire 145

Dinosaurs & Cowboys - Dan Madigan 151

Curse of the Undead - Phoef Sutton 157

7 Faces of Dr. Lao - Steven Peros 161

Billy the Kid vs. Dracula - Mike Peros 165

Jesse James Meets Frankenstein's Daughter - Tracy Mercer 169

 TOC

STEVEN PEROS

Welcome to our third book in this series. First, there was *Giant Bug Cinema*, covering the world of very big ants, grasshoppers, spiders, et al, from the 1930's to 1968, the end of the purported "Monster Kid" era. I contributed two chapters to editor Mark Bailey's mad fever dream and then partnered with him to select the writers, edit, and contribute to the second book, *Giant Beast Cinema*, which covered everything else that was unnaturally giganticized on movie screens during the same period that was not a bug (octopi, bats, gorillas, etc).

After both books landed in Amazon's Top Ten for Sci-fi Movie books, my desire was to then move on to follow-up volumes for both books, taking us into the 1970's, 80's, and beyond for both Bugs and Beasts. But that sneaky Mark Bailey had other cinemaniacal plans afoot. As far as he was concerned, there were more fantastic films to mine from the same Monster Kid era. What of the killer plants, insisted Mark? The Weird Westerns? And of course, the outside-the-box aliens?

To prove to me that there were enough outrageous outliers to constitute a third Monster Kid era book, Mark submitted a list of movies to me that, dagnabbit, I found myself adding to. And thus, *Cinema Bizarro* was born.

With more titles being covered this time around, we had to expand our outreach beyond our mostly available writers from *Giant Beast*: Larry Blamire, Tracy Mercer, Mike Peros, Brian R. Solomon (our resident *kaiju* expert), and yours truly (our contributor bios follow this Introduction). Adding to the mix were two-time Emmy winner, Phoef Sutton, who was such a fan of our earlier books that he let his interest in contributing to this new volume be known; controversial and erudite WWE scribe/producer, Dan Madigan, whose self-professed love of "any movie with a ninja, monkey, or midget" made him a perfect choice; and Nadia Robertson, whose presence within these pages is the result of using social media for the forces of good. We discovered her loving scribbles on all things monstrously bizarre via Facebook and offered her five chapters, as we did the others. Rounding out the contributor roster is Mark Bailey and our Co-Editor, Steven Orkin, with one chapter a piece.

This time around, I gave each writer the complete list of 38 movies and told them to send me a list of the top 10 they'd like to write about in descending order. My hope was to give each of them at least three titles from their top 5 or top 10. It worked out perfectly. But then, of course, Larry Blamire had the audacity to remind us that there were a host of low budget Weird Westerns from the 1930's and 40's we hadn't considered. We could not write individual chapters on each title so it was decided Larry would write double-length chapters on each decade, discussing over a dozen such movies in each chapter in his inimitably passionate, informed, and dryly funny style.

As a result, I can safely say that I learned about more movies heretofore unknown to me in this book than the other two books put together. Not only via Larry's Weird Western Roundup chapters (which should each win their own Pulitzer!), but other titles that slipped through my personal radar over the years, like *The Woman Eater*, *Brides of Blood*, *Warning from Space*, *The Bubble*, and the far-better-than-expected vampire western, *Curse of the Undead*. And just as I wrote in revisionist fashion in our last book, extolling the virtues of the much-maligned

The Giant Claw, Phoef Sutton sheds newfound positive light on *Robot Monster*, while my film journalist brother Mike extolls the unheralded qualities of both *Invisible Invaders* and *Billy the Kid vs. Dracula*. And for me, it was a pleasure to complete my writing on the three exceptional Quatermass movies from Hammer Films, the brainchild of the singular Nigel Kneale.

The great news for all of you is that every bizarre movie detailed in this book is available to rent, purchase, or stream (most for free!). So be sure to have a notepad ready and – if you must – dog-ear the title of interest so you can immediately screen the insanity the moment you complete each chapter.

Just know that everything you thought you knew about fantastic cinema will be altered upon the completion of your journey through these pages. You can thank us or curse us, but I recommend letting *Cinema Bizarro* envelop you in its loving embrace like the cool, slimy clutches of *The Blob*.

"You're next! You're next!"

The Authors
In Order of Appearance

Dan Madigan has worked in everything your parents warned about - horror movies, professional wrestling, and rock & roll, the triumvirate of taboo and trouble. While creating the horror franchise *See No Evil* for Lionsgate Films and the *WWE*, Madigan was also instrumental behind the camera in writing, producing and directing *RAW* and *Smackdown*, the *WWE*'s weekly wrestling shows. Madigan wrote the critically acclaimed book *Mondo Lucha A Go-Go* for HarperCollins, the definitive tome on Mexican wrestling, and there have been several documentaries created based his book. After working in nightclubs and bars at sixteen, and a stint on the carnival midway, and then an extended stay with Disney Animation, Madigan became the road manager for the legendary rock/jazz fusion band "Blood, Sweat & Tears" and other musical acts. Madigan found himself traveling around the world before finally settling down to concentrate on his writing.

Tracy Mercer is an Emmy-nominated TV and Film executive-turned-producer who has worked on projects including Ang Lee's *Hulk*, *Aeon Flux*, *Invictus*, *Five Flights Up*, the CBS hit series *Madam Secretary*, and Brad Anderson's low-fi sci-fi thriller, *Worldbreaker*. She was a contributor to *Giant Beast Cinema* and is also the co-host of the irreverent film buff comedy podcast, *My Favorite Shtty Movie*, which can be watched on both its Facebook and YouTube show pages, with the audio version available for downloading anywhere you find your podcasts. Tracy is a third generation Angeleno and second generation

 5

cinephile who was weaned on equal parts Universal Monster films, 1950's sci-fi classics, and campy midnight movies. Among her proudest achievements: being sent to the Principal's office in 3rd grade for making her flip-book version of the *Alien* chest-burster scene and earning her brown belt in Tae Kwon Do. She currently resides in Los Angeles with her rescue mutt, Snake Plissken.

Mike Peros is the author of the recent, well-received Hollywood biographies *Dan Duryea: Heel with a Heart* and *Jose Ferrer: Success and Survival*, both published by the University Press of Mississippi. He was a contributor to *Giant Beast Cinema* and also writes film reviews for *NoHoArtsDistrict.com*, where he tries to steer readers to films that might have otherwise escaped their attention (while also occasionally reviewing the studio blockbuster). When he's not watching or writing about movies, Mike can be found in Brooklyn as the English Department Chair at Bishop Loughlin Memorial High School. Perhaps his favorite movie monster is Christopher Plummer's unsettling, all-too-inhuman psychopath in *The Silent Partner.*

Larry Blamire is a writer, director, actor, artist and playwright known for the feature films, *The Lost Skeleton of Cadavra*, *Trail of the Screaming Forehead*, *The Lost Skeleton Returns Again*, and *Dark and Stormy Night*, and is writer-creator of the *Mark Time Award*-winning *Big Dan Frater* audio series. His books (at Lulu.com) include *Doc Armstrong: Suburb at the Edge of Never*, two western-horror collections (*Tales of the Callamo Mountains*), and volumes of surreal cartoons. Larry won the Boston Theatre Critics Circle Award for Best Actor and is a published playwright whose *Robin Hood* has been performed worldwide. His epic graphic novel, *Steam Wars* (*steamwars.com*), will soon be an RPG from Onyx Path, for whom he regularly writes/illustrates. This unrepentant Monster Kid was a contributor to *Giant Beast Cinema*, numerous Blu-ray commentaries, and is the proud recipient of three Rondo Awards, including for his column in *Video Watchdog*. Larry currently writes for *bare•bones Magazine*, is developing a comic, *Flapjack Alley*, and can be found hiding under his own name on Facebook, Twitter, and Instagram.

Nadia Robertson started a lifelong love affair with cinema in her early childhood. After stealing the family handicam to make her own

THE AUTHORS

movies, she knew what she wanted to do when she grew up. Nadia achieved a bachelor's degree in Theater & Film and has since worked professionally on and off camera within all various aspects of the TV/Film industry since 2010 in cities across the country. Her passion for cinema extends to writing on the subject in any online forum or printed publication that will have her - including contributing articles for magazines such as *Cinema Macabre*, *Delirium*, and *We Belong Dead*, as well as hosting her own podcast, *Cinema Chats*, and guest appearing on many others. Lately, Nadia can be seen making movie magic happen as an actor in Atlanta, alongside operating as a filmmaker for 25 years under her company, 1931 Productions.

Phoef Sutton is a screenwriter and NY Times bestselling novelist who was born in Washington D.C. He won two Emmys and a Golden Globe for the TV series *Cheers*. He also wrote for *Boston Legal* and the cult hit *Terriers*. He produced *Darrow & Darrow* and *Chesapeake Shores* for the Hallmark Channel. His novels include *Fifteen Minutes to Live*, *Crush*, *Heart Attack and Vine*, *Colorado Boulevard*, and *From Away*. He lives in South Pasadena, California and Vinalhaven, Maine.

Brian R. Solomon is a pop culture and film writer with more than 25 years experience. He was a contributor to *Giant Beast Cinema* and is also the author of six books on sports and entertainment, including the award-winning *Blood and Fire: The Unbelievable Real-Life Story of Wrestling's Original Sheik*, as well as *Godzilla FAQ*, the comprehensive reference guide for the Big G. His love affair with *kaiju* began back in the late '70s thanks to the monster movie marathons on WOR Channel 9 in New York City, and he'll always have a soft spot for *Godzilla vs. The Smog Monster* and, yes, *Godzilla's Revenge*. Brian has also worked extensively within the pro wrestling business, including seven years with *WWE*, spending his time among a different breed of angry, fighting giants. He's also a podcaster and reporter, as well as an English teacher with a master's specialization in Shakespeare. He is the proud father of three, and lives in Trumbull, Connecticut with his wife and youngest son.

Mark Bailey is a monster movie/bad film historian, amateur animator, and filmmaker hobbyist. He conceived, co-edited, and designed the previous books in this series *Giant Bug Cinema - A Monster Kid's*

Guide and *Giant Beast Cinema - A Monstrous Movie Guide*. His presentations *Giant Monsters Attack NYC - A History*, *Bad Film a Go Go*, and *Giant Bug Cinema - A Creature-Feature History* have been successfully presented at *BoroughCon*, *EternalCon*, *GalaxyCon*, *GFest*, *ICon*, and *WinterCon*. He is also the creator/curator of the *New York City Giant Monster Attack Map* (*nycgmam.com*). While currently teaching graphic design to high schoolers, he lives in North Jersey with his brilliant and lovely wife Kara (Hrabosky) and feline overlords Ella, Griffin, and Roxie.

Steven B. Orkin is a near-lifelong resident of Long Island with a passion for storytelling and the craft of writing. He has provided editorial contributions to all three books in this series and is the author of the novellas, *Susie* and *The Lost 95*, both available through Amazon and Smashwords. Steve was a winner of Stephen King's On Writing contest, from his wonderful memoir / writing guide of the same name. You can learn more about him at his website: *starren.wixsite.com/stevenorkin*.

Steven Peros is an award-winning filmmaker and comic-book writer whose debut Rondo Award-nominated graphic novel, *Stoker & Wells*, is being developed for TV by the former President of Marvel Studios at his company, Amasia. Steven wrote *The Cat's Meow*, starring Kirsten Dunst and directed by Peter Bogdanovich, one-hour dramas for NBC, MTV, and wrote for AMC's Emmy-winning series, *The Lot*. Steven was a writer on Disney's *Around the World in 80 Days*, starring Jackie Chan, and wrote *A Country Christmas Story*, co-starring Dolly Parton. As a film journalist, Steven wrote the biography, *H.M. Wynant: You Must Believe!*, was an editor and contributor to *Giant Beast Cinema*, and articles for *MovieMaker*, *Village Voice*, *Scr(i)pt*, and others. He has contributed BluRay commentary tracks for many classic films and is an avid 16mm film and movie poster collector. For his social media links and contact information, please visit *stevenperos.com*.

A Note From Mark Bailey

I'm the monster movie nerd who conceived and helped bring our first two books, *Giant Bug Cinema - A Monster Kid's Guide* and *Giant Beast Cinema - A Monstrous Movie Guide*, into a reality. What still leaves me speechless is that our first book almost never happened, yet here we are on our third in the series. What an incredible journey of creativity and collaboration! This time around, along with overall design, artistic, and layout responsibilities, I tried my hand at writing a chapter (*Venus Flytrap*). I hope you enjoy it as much as I did writing it. FYI: aspiring wordsmiths, writing is incredibly hard. While I have the privilege of working yet again with Steven Peros and Steve Orkin, I'm also delighted to have repeat collaborations with Larry Blamire, Tracy Mercer, Mike Peros, Brian R. Solomon. They all brought the same level of creativity while offering new ideas to help ensure a successful finished product. And our first-time contributors Dan Madigan, Nadia Robertson, and Phoef Sutton have added some extraordinary work to such a wonderfully niche collection as this.

A Note From Steven B. Orkin

I greatly enjoyed working on this third installment of our charming little film guide series. Having the opportunity to edit the work of our contributors (to say nothing of standing amongst them as a fellow contributor) was a great honor, and their excellent writing skills made my copyediting job easy!

Though I have a great passion for film (particularly genre films) and storytelling, I wouldn't consider myself a cinephile. Because of this, I continue to learn a great deal about a unique part of film history, as well as individual films, in the context of working on the 'Cinema' books with my two near-lifelong chums, Steve Peros and Mark Bailey. Steve's primary editing and fact-checking skills remain impeccable, and Mark's graphic design and organizational skills are equally impressive. It's been a pleasure to be part of this project!

THE THING FROM ANOTHER WORLD
1951

DAN MADIGAN

Six years after that little skirmish called The Second World War had finished, the release of *The Thing From Another World* hit the theaters. The world was still on shaky ground, suspicions ran deep, and fears even deeper. The anxiety over Nazi barbarity and the militaristic savagery of the Japanese were replaced with something far more insidious: the terror of all-growing, all-soul-stealing Communism. It seemed our former allies, the Russians, were now our political antagonists. Their way of life - austere, authoritarian, and totalitarian - was fundamentally against everything we as a democracy stood for. The Russian ideology of high-tech Bolshevism was something to strike dread in the most ardent hearts of American patriots.

The subtext in this film is not subtle. It's right in your face, like a cold blast of arctic wind. It isn't a cautionary tale hinting about the Red Scare, but an admonitory declaration for the Scarlet Panic that was potentially threatening to infiltrate our American way of life, and not just by foreign invaders from outer space, but something far worse: home-grown terrestrial Marxists.

Financed by maverick filmmaker Howard Hawks' Winchester Pictures Corporation, the film was released by RKO Radio Pictures. Hawks himself brought a rousing sense of adventure to the stories he wrote and directed. Having served as a lieutenant during the First World War in the Aviation Section, U.S. Signal Corps, he knew first-hand what military know-how could do to overcome adversity in dire situations, and in *The Thing From Another World*, he'd put that knowledge to good use.

The genesis of this story comes from the August 1938 issue of *Astounding Science Fiction* magazine, which published the novella "Who Goes There?" by John W. Campbell (under the pseudonym Don A. Stuart). With its taut script by multi-Tony winner, Charles Lederer (child prodigy and nephew to William Randolph Hearst's mistress Marion Davis) and the uncredited duo of Howard Hawks and twice Oscar-winner Ben Hecht, the talent behind the story is top tier terrific.

Kenneth Tobey, the dauntless military hero in other classic sci-fi films of the decade, such as *The Beast from 20,000 Fathoms* (1953) and *It Came from Beneath the Sea* (1955), stars as Captain Patrick Hendry, leader of a seasoned and salty crew of airmen who, along with a group of research scientists lead by Dr. Arthur Carrington (Robert Cornthwaite) discover a spaceship freshly frozen in the Arctic ice and bring back one of its occupants to their base camp with disastrous defrosting results. With a cast of great supporting character actors and a truly horrifying villain in the lumbering, cold-blooded, alien Thing (menacingly portrayed by future television western star, James Arness of *Gunsmoke* fame), *The Thing From Another World* starts off the 50's sci-fi craze with the highest of marks.

The movie speeds along at a fast clip, with the typical Hawksian style of fast pacing, snappy dialogue, and tough professionalism displayed by both male and female characters working under duress. However, this picture was not directed by Howard Hawks but by his friend and frequent editor, Christian Nyby. There have been unsubstantiated rumors milling around since its release that first-time director Nyby didn't direct the film at all, that in reality, it was actually Hawks himself. Nyby had worked closely with Hawks since 1945, editing several of Hawks' more famous films (*To Have and Have Not*, *The Big Sleep*, and *Red River*), so who better would know how Hawks paced his films? He emulated his friend and was right there watching him work so it's only natural that his first time out, he'd rely on the style he'd studied so well. However, Nyby's output subsequent to *The Thing From Another World* never reached the mastery of his first foray behind the camera.

Off-screen, Hawks would encourage actors to ad-lib to get realistic reactions from their fellow cast members and, along with naturalistic dialogue and overlapping banter, there is a vérité feel to their plight. The script's comedic touches, subtle-to-gallows humor, are peppered throughout the tightly-constructed story and serve as release valves for the pressures that are mounting against Captain Hendry and his crew.

The Thing is a seemingly unstoppable, highly intelligent adversary from outer space, who is basically a hulking leguminous blood-sucker with lousy interplanetary social skills who sees warm-blooded humans as nothing more than mulch. It's a cross between a mute Count Dracula and an anthropomorphic zucchini, and its main goal is to drain everyone of their blood to fertilize his own growing army of little things to advance an invasion of earth. The premise is simple, the execution brilliant.

But if battling this vampiric vegetable wasn't bad enough, Hendry is in constant conflict with Dr. Carrington, who wears a grey turtleneck sweater, sports a sharp, Van Dyke beard, and dons a Russian-style fur cap, clearly the aesthetic of the intellectual liberal or the downtrodden beatnik, both enemies of the red-blooded American way of life in the 1950's. What is the cause of this dispute? Dr. Carrington, extremely intelligent with a slight touch of Asperger's Syndrome and a big dose of narcissistic personality disorder, wants to keep the newly-defrosted space visitor alive at all costs to garner as much of its interplanetary knowledge as he can. Captain Hendry's motivations are more on a practical level — his self-preservation, the survival of his crew, and averting the violent exsanguination of the entire human race.

Some of the set pieces in *The Thing From Another World* have become legendary in Hollywood history. The shot of men standing on the ice in a circle, realizing they've discovered a flying saucer, the Thing battling a pack of sled dogs, the Thing engulfed in a ball of fire and jumping through a window to escape, and just wait until Captain Hendry opens the door to the greenhouse a second time. All of these clearly show the technical proficiency and artistic skill that six-time Academy

CINEMA BIZARRO

Award nominee, Russel Harlan brought to the picture's cinematography.

The beautiful Margret Sheridan received top billing in her first movie as Nikki Nicholson, Dr. Carrington's faithful secretary and Captain Hendry's kinky love interest (handcuffs, anyone?). Sheridan was discovered by Hawks himself and became his "protégé in training", but marriage and motherhood came first in her life, so while the promising career that Hawks had planned for her did not pan out, her role as the strong, loyal, and dependable Nikki will last in our collective cinematic imaginations.

Filling out the story is an unsettling but brilliant score created by Russian-born musical maestro, Dimitri Tiomkin, whose credits on Hollywood classics are too numerous to list here. This twenty-two-time nominated composer won four Oscars in his long career and *The Thing From Another World* stands out as one of his best.

And for closing lines in Hollywood history, of all the memorable last words uttered in filmdom, none are more haunting than reporter Ned Scott (Douglas Spencer) warning to a room full of reporters, *"Every one of you listening to my voice, tell the world, tell this to everybody wherever they are. Watch the skies. Everywhere. Keep looking. Keep watching the skies."* So, the first volley of human defiance toward other-worldly, would-be conquerors was fired, the invaders bested and beaten by American ingenuity and patriotic fervor.

Of course, I'd be remiss if I didn't mention, the once unjustly lambasted, now rightly lauded, John Carpenter masterpiece reimagining of *The Thing*. His 1982 take on Campbell's source material keeps closer to the original feel of the story, with growing paranoia amongst a team of scientists. The continually transmuting, all-flesh consuming monstrosity is brought to life by the practical special effects genius of 22-year-old Rob Bottin, who keeps the Thing as the original, indescribable, Lovecraftian abomination it is.

INVASION OF THE BODY SNATCHERS

1956

TRACY MERCER

To this day, I can't glimpse a Brussel Sprout without having a visceral childhood memory of being scared. Not even the lure of sautéing said Brussel Sprouts with bacon can alleviate this (perhaps?) irrational fear. Let me explain. My adolescent terror of being 'snatched' in my sleep by a nefarious force didn't start with *A Nightmare on Elm Street*'s (1984) iconic Freddie Krueger. Instead, it all began a few years earlier when my sci-fi buff father rented Don Siegel's 1956 science fiction masterpiece *Invasion of the Body Snatchers* for my then grade school self.

This briskly paced, gorgeous, film noir-styled flick serves up a dose of pure cinematic paranoia that's as effective today as it was on upon its initial release during McCarthy Era America. Based on Jack Finney's 1954 science fiction novel, *The Body Snatchers*, the film takes place in a quaint, sleepy California town named Santa Mira where everything

CINEMA BIZARRO

looks like a Rockwellian Saturday Evening Post pictorial. Only, there seems to be an unexplained uptick in friends, families, and neighbors seeming a little 'off' to those closest to them. "She's not my mother!" "That's not my husband!" become common refrains as we learn there have been a series of appointments made with hunky Kevin McCarthy's small-town doc, Miles Bennell. Several patients claim their loved ones just don't seem to be themselves. A man of science, Miles attempts to explain away patients' concerns as being just a crazy number of Capgras Delusion cases (a very real-world affliction where one believes a loved one has been replaced by an imposter).

To be fair, Miles is also distracted by his former girlfriend/love of his life, Becky, who has recently returned to Santa Mira, a newly divorced woman played by the absolutely stunning Dana Wynter. The romantic sparks between McCarthy's Miles and Wynter's Becky are palpable and add a juicy love story into this delicious sci-fiction/horror mix. Their screen chemistry and relationship feels more contemporary and less chaste than other films of the era. We get to see Wynter wearing jeans (!) while cooking breakfast for McCarthy the morning after they've spent the night together and she even gets to save Miles by stabbing a "pod person" at one critical point. Her worldly Becky is a sexy example of a gal who keeps her wits about her, has agency, and helps Miles put the pieces of the film's mystery together. As an aside — Kate Capshaw's Willie Scott in *Indiana Jones and the Temple of Doom* (1984) made 28 years later would have been cooler if she had been written to be more like Becky. Or even, *Raiders of the Lost Ark*'s Marion. But, that's a conversation for another book.

Now, we can't go any further without talking about the term "Pod Person". Yes, *Invasion of the Body Snatchers* is the genesis of that still common-in-use cultural reference. As Siegel's film unravels the mystery behind Santa Mira's strange community behavior, we learn that alien plant spores have fallen from space onto this town and started to flower into large pods. These pods look like – you guessed it – elongated Brussel Sprouts! What makes them nightmare fuel, you ask? Well, if a person falls asleep in proximity to these pods, the pods will give birth to an imposter that replicates the memories and physical attributes of its human host. The terrible difference between the imposter and the now deceased human it replaces? The pod people are devoid of human emotion. While at first blush, the idea of no fear, no grief, and a 'chill' existence might sound like pluses, the assimilation into an emotional sameness also means there is no LOVE. That's right, there is NO love possible in Pod World. Bad timing for Miles and Becky to be sure.

The film continues to clip along at a pace many contemporary films would rightly envy and delivers more than its share of dark comedy and killer set pieces. Bubbling pods (don't look too close or it might seem like dish soap!) spitting out gooey bodies that slowly grow finger prints and other person-specific details. Authority figures turning on those they swore to serve and protect abound! Why, even the operators won't let you call out of town. A growing sense of doom that perhaps Miles and Becky are among the last to not be infected serves as a ticking clock because as the audience, we know that our two lovebirds can't stay awake forever. Sleep equals death. Miles and Becky take what is probably speed to keep them awake while they work up a survival plan.

Their efforts include bravely walking amongst the pod people, trying to act with no emotion as they plot an escape from Santa Mira with the hope of alerting authorities outside small town America to a threat that could overtake the country… and our world. Attempting to act like pod people is a great plan until Becky sees a dog almost hit by a truck and screams, which alerts the pod people they are still very human. A race for survival ensues!

There is a reason *Invasion of the Body Snatchers* has been remade (to date) 3 times. Pods just may be the metaphor for all seasons… I mean eras! 1978's *Invasion of the Body Snatchers*, directed by The *Right Stuff*'s Philip Kaufman is set in San Francisco and is a post-Watergate paranoia era thriller starring the late Donald Sutherland as Dr. Bennell. It's also one of the all-time best remakes in cinema. 1993's version was called *Body Snatchers* (directed by *Bad Lieutenant*'s Abel Ferrara) and plays almost like a reaction to the first US Iraqi invasion in 1991. Set primarily on a military base, it uses the pod person metaphor to tell us something about the Military Industrial Complex. The arguably least creatively successful version of Finney's tale is director Oliver Hirschbiegel's *The Invasion* (2007) starring a gender swapped version of therapist Dr. Bennell in the form of Nicole Kidman, who is on the run with a pre-James Bond Daniel Craig. This last version is remark-

CINEMA BIZARRO

able for removing the pods from the pod person film (hey, Hollywood development doesn't always get it right!). But to be fair, post global COVID pandemic, the concept of spreading space spores in a vaccine to make the assimilation go viral may play differently to contemporary audiences.

We should also note a fun movie-buff factoid regarding the fictional location of Santa Mira for the under-appreciated, body-replicating gem that is *Halloween 3: Season of the Witch*. Santa Mira is the name that Tommy Lee Wallace's 1982 film gives to the location of Silver Shamrock, the evil company that makes that film's sadistic Halloween masks that figure prominently in the movie. The filmmakers were such fans of Siegel's *Invasion of the Body Snatchers*, they paid homage by embracing his fictional town's name into their film. Both films also used California's Sierra Madre as locations.

In 1994, Siegel's film was selected for preservation in the US National Film Registry by the Library of Congress because it is "culturally, historically, or aesthetically significant." While many still feel Siegel was making a political statement about McCarthyism, he had this to say: "I felt that this was a very important story. I think that the world is populated by pods and I wanted to show them. I think so many people have no feeling about cultural things, no feeling of pain, of sorrow. The political reference to Senator McCarthy and totalitarianism was inescapable but I tried not to emphasize it because I feel that motion pictures are primarily to entertain and I did not want to preach."

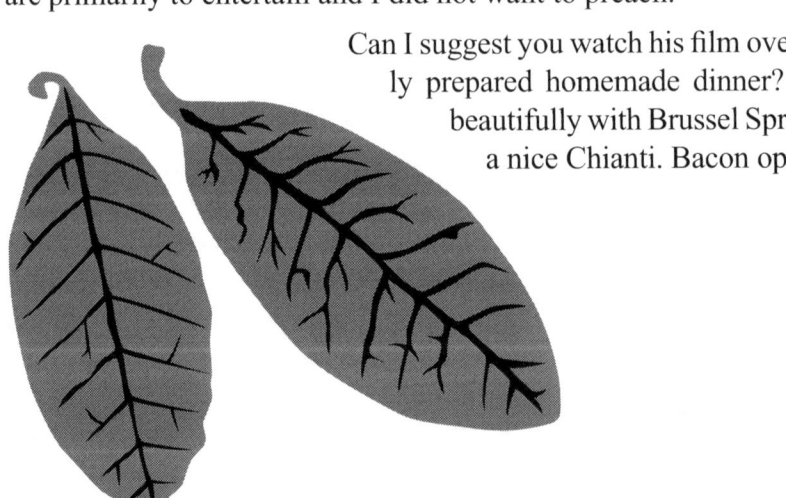

Can I suggest you watch his film over a nicely prepared homemade dinner? It pairs beautifully with Brussel Sprouts and a nice Chianti. Bacon optional.

1957

MIKE PEROS

1957's *From Hell It Came* is a prime example of that rare type of horror film, one in which the major threat is a tree monster. This type of creature had appeared previously—notably the apple tree that frightens Dorothy in 1939's *The Wizard of Oz*. When you examine the occasional "tree monster" movie, the creature's key advantage is the element of surprise. Tree monsters, as in the possessed tree in 1981's *Evil Dead* or 1982's *Poltergeist*, can wreak havoc because they appear to be ordinary trees; unwitting victims don't realize they're in danger until it's too late. What distinguishes *From Hell It Came* is that midway through the film, *everyone* is aware that there is a possessed, killer tree on the move — yet this doesn't stop the tree from racking up victims. I say *still* because if you've ever seen a "killer tree" movie, these are lumbering creatures, moving ever so slowly (you rarely see a tree sprint), so that all a prospective victim needs to do is run swiftly (or even walk briskly) to escape. However, several characters reach an untimely end in *From Hell It Came* because of a shuffling stump. Without going out on a limb, let's discover why...

Working from a debut screenplay by Richard Bernstein, *From Hell It Came* was the second feature from John Milner and brother Dan, both former film editors who had recently branched out into production, with 1955's *Phantom from 10,000 Leagues* serving as their inaugural effort. Dan directed *Phantom...* and again took on the directorial duties here. *From Hell It Came* takes place on an unnamed South Seas Island where white scientists live in uneasy proximity to the island natives. Prince Kimo (Gregg Palmer) is about to be executed for poisoning his father, the island Chief. It's clear that unsavory witch doctor Tano (Robert Swan) and new Chief, Maranka (Baynes Barron) have framed Kimo. (These "tough-guy" natives are angry that Kino has been working with U.S. scientists who have set up shop nearby. Kimo pleads with his wife Korey (Suzanne Ridgway) to save him, but she turns on Kimo too, since she now believes herself to be Maranka's woman. The enraged Kimo vows to return from the grave: "I promise you. I'll come back from Hell and make you pay!" With that, Tano drives a dagger into Kimo's heart, and he is buried in a hollow tree trunk.

Meanwhile, the scientists, led by Dr. Arnold (played by Tod Andrews, a capable stage and screen actor whose credits include the lead role in *Mister Roberts* during the play's first road tour) and John McNamara's Professor Clark, have been medically treating plague-ridden islanders while investigating the remote possibility of radioactivity as a cause. Though the film doesn't follow up on the ramifications (especially since radioactivity is quickly discounted), there is some attempt, in this unpretentious 1950's sci-fi, to address the tensions inherent in both American colonialism and the possible misuse of nuclear power... but I digress. Though Dr. Arnold helps the natives, he wants to return to the States, but then, Dr. Terry Mason (Tina Carver) arrives. He's sweet on her, she's sweet on him, but she has her career to think about, and is not ready to conform to societal expectations and be just a "doctor's wife." Dr. Mason also wants to remain on that island and be of some help—though that becomes questionable, to say the least.

 20

FROM HELL IT CAME

After the earth moves around Kimo's grave, an already-adult tree begins to grow. Dr. Arnold and Dr. Mason are rightly concerned, especially after Kimo's friend, Norgu (Lee Rhodes), one of the few natives who believe in "white medicine," tells the tale of a native chief who returned from the dead as a 'tree monster' called "Tabonga." (Note: spellings abound for this creature, but I'll take Tabonga.) According to Norgu, Tabonga roamed the island, killing numerous people, before eventually disappearing.

As the new stump grows, it develops a furrowed brow and an effective scowl, while sprouting a ceremonial dagger, green blood—and a beating heart. Much of the credit for this creation goes to the uncredited visual effects designer Paul Blaisdell, who performed similar wonders on a number of 50's sci-fi films like *The Beast With a Million Eyes* (1955) and *The She Creature* (1957). Producers Dan and John Milner tweaked Blaisdell's original design so that Tabonga became a little shorter, and squatter, with (also uncredited) actor Chester Hayes inside the rubber-suited "monster" to maneuver it.

Despite Norgu's warnings, the intrepid scientists uproot the stump, though Dr. Mason is worried "it knows what we're saying." Later, Dr. Arnold is all for tossing the ailing stump into the quicksand, but Dr. Mason wants to keep it alive. Faster than you can say "I meddled in things that Man must leave alone," she injects it with a life-saving formula. Witch doctor Tano foolishly thinks he can turn Tabonga into his servant to kill all the whites (Did Tano forget Kimo's earlier vow—not to mention the telltale dagger sticking out of its trunk?). Luckily, the discarded Korey overhears this threat and warns the scientists—as a reject from Team Maranka, she now wants to be on the whites' side.

A rejuvenated Tabonga escapes and when we see it next, it is moving laboriously across the landscape—it's a trunk with a mission. Simultaneously, an aggrieved Korey attacks Maranka's new gal, Naomi (Tani Marsh), but Naomi is unwilling to be killed and momentarily stuns Korey, who falls conveniently into the movable branches of Tabonga, which summarily hurls her into the quicksand. So far, so credible, at least as tree monster murders go. But then, Chief Maranka sees Tabonga, throws a spear at the advancing stump—and then backs away, slowly, into another tree, where he is caught and throttled to death by

CINEMA BIZARRO

Tabonga (The option to run is one the Chief does not take). Back at the science hut, while Dr. Mason is none too happy that the creature is on a killing spree, she is relieved it is still alive. Got to wonder about her…

Tabonga then stalks Tano, who cleverly lures the creature into a pit, which the natives set on fire. The burned Tabonga is nothing if not persistent and climbs from the pit, so the frightened natives do the sensible thing—they *run* (They also plead for help from the scientists, having realized the folly of following Tano). Tabonga spots a terrified Tano, who quickly stumbles over a tree trunk (irony, anyone?). After Tabonga swiftly dispatches Tano, it grabs Dr. Mason (who has also backed into it—people should really *look* where they're going). The leads take turns firing at the Terry-wielding Tabonga (hoping to hit the dagger, not Terry) with Dr. Arnold making the winning shot, striking the dagger, and driving it into Tabonga's heart.

An early reviewer of *From Hell It Came* quipped "And to Hell it can go." That has always seemed a little harsh; however, for a seventy-one-minute film about a killer tree, there is some dead wood in *From Hell It Came*. The pacing is uneven, with excessive exposition, lengthy native dancing, unnecessary comic relief (courtesy of Linda Watkins' man-hungry, trading post owner), and tedious romantic scenes bogging down the first half. However, once Kimo returns from the dead as Tabonga, the movie comes alive, as the aggrieved Tabonga takes the law into its own branches, resulting in the first-of-its-kind "tree-hunt thriller".

Besides the undeniable entertainment value, *From Hell It Came* also provides a valuable public service on how *not* to react when danger slowly comes your way. Watch and learn…

THE UNKNOWN TERROR

1957

LARRY BLAMIRE

"There's always a bottom... Just depends on how deep it is." *The Unknown Terror* is one of those tight little movies boxed-up in a soundstage that asks you to cut it some slack and suspend your disbelief. I never saw this one as a Monster Kid, but it falls into a category near and dear to my heart: the Science Fiction Expedition. *The Land Unknown*, *Lost Continent* and *The Cyclops* all lured me in with their promises of adventure and the unknown.

A pre-credit sequence shows Charles Gray (a regular of director Charles Marquis Warren, later on the Warren-created *Rawhide* TV series) crawling through a cave and halting with a look of terror. This poor fellow turns out to be Gina Matthews' (Mala Powers) brother, who vanished exploring the Cueva de la Muerte (Cave of the Dead). Now, Gina and her wealthy husband Dan (John Howard) are outfitting an expedition to find him. Spelunker Pete Morgan (Paul Richards), whose leg was permanently injured saving Dan's life, and who has a history with Gina, unexpectedly volunteers to come along. There's every indication that this "love triangle" (a device that's frankly trite and overdone) will breed tension, even treachery, but writer Kenneth Higgins and director Warren are too smart for that. These characters are essentially decent people who happen to have a past, but manage to rise above it to accomplish a task.

John Howard (best remembered for *The Philadelphia Story* and portraying *Bulldog Drummond*) gives the millionaire integrity and drive, while lovely Mala Powers, who I shall forever link in the Mala-Mara-Marla trio of 1950s science fiction heroines (shame on you if you can't name them), gives Gina sincere credibility. Whether playing good guys or bad, Paul Richards always had a certain edginess, and it works here as this gutsy, handicapped man, anxious to prove himself.

Having the clues to the cave's location embedded in a calypso song is an imaginative touch, particularly when sung by the acclaimed Sir Lancelot from Val Lewton's *I Walked with a Zombie*. The expedition's other ace-in-the-cave (ouch) is nervous and reluctant native Raoul Koom (Richard Gilden), a member of the (somewhat generic) jungle village they're heading to. Much to his confusion, he is warmly welcomed by his people. But when he's absorbed into the happy crowd, only to disappear, it's strangely unnerving, and even more ominous when the smiles abruptly vanish from the villagers' faces, adding to the shroud of mystery.

We meet Dr. Ramsey somewhat inauspiciously, toiling over a pot of boiling… something… looking more short-order cook than Charles Laughton's incongruously elegant Dr. Moreau. As portrayed by Gerald Milton, he's a working-class scientist, more surly than mad, with the build of a linebacker. Milton, who had a busy career playing thugs, gangsters, and western baddies, is certainly an interesting and unexpected choice. When he takes a whip to his poor native wife Concha (May Wynn) for a simple accident, we see his dark side, not unlike Walter Huston's self-appointed jungle lord Flint in the grim, pre-code *Kongo* (1932). In fact, he shares Flint's delusion of jungle domination, proudly announcing his use of "mumbo jumbo" on the natives, as a result of which he's treated "like a spiritual king… and I like it."

In response to our heroes' inquiry about the Cave of the Dead, he flatly states "No caves around here," then amusingly backtracks when they mention Cueva de la Muerte (Ohhhhh… *that* cave of the dead).

When asked where it is, he ambiguously states, "That's their purgatory… You go… *this* way" and moves his spoon ominously down to the flames beneath the pot. Of course, just whom he's referring to will later be revealed when the explorers encounter the cave's strange denizens. At first, Ramsey claims to be canning his own fruit, but the breaking of one of his jars assures us we will never buy preserves from this guy, as its hissing bubbling contents spread over the floor. He confesses he's working with "fungal slime molds" for the development of antibiotics, ominously observing "a remarkable fungus… You can actually see it grow."

The first horror comes on an appropriately stormy night, and it's a memorable scene. Concha tells them about voices coming from underground (an eerie idea, for starters) and Dan and Pete decide to investigate, leaving Gina home alone. An alarming wide shot reveals the back of a figure lurching toward the building in a crash of thunder and lightning. It then proceeds to watch Gina through the bedroom window (will women in horror movies never learn about mirrors and dressing tables?). Even though we don't see it up close, we are able to make out distorted features; enough to provoke that Mala Powers scream and send her running from the hacienda into the jungle, where the thing chases her. Now, as much as I get the whole the-less-you-see-the-creepier-it-is logic, the Monster Kid in me is yelling for a monster closeup (don't even get me started on *World Without End*). Hey, even a quick insert if the makeup doesn't hold up. Alas, it is not to be (What Charles, no coverage?). Still, the tense stalking of Gina through the underbrush, and its culmination, is one of the film's highlights.

I think the biggest difference resulting from Imprint's lovely Blu-ray, vs. the old TV pan-and-scan, is in the cave scenes, at last presented in Regalscope (B-movie mogul Robert Lippert's black-and-white answer to Fox's "color only" CinemaScope), where they are much better appreciated. The rampant crawling trails of deadly fungi are no doubt some kind of suds on steroids, but the overall visual effect is fairly satisfying. Add to that some quite decent cavern sets (anyone else think of *Caltiki – the Immortal Monster* when they see that bubbling underground pool?), under the talented eye of prolific cinematographer Joseph Biroc, whose crisp lighting and camera make the fungal walls pleasingly grotesque in black-and-white.

CINEMA BIZARRO

I cannot figure why people keep trusting Ramsey's right-hand man Lino, the least-convincing native in the movie (played by dependable Western actor, Duane Grey). After he bails on the heroes once, you'd think they'd know better. But as Pete and Gina return to the cave to rescue Dan, they give this guy another chance. To reward their confidence, he tries to blow them up with dynamite, but ends up taking a boulder shower. When Pete and Gina make their way into the inner chamber, we are greeted by what looks startlingly like a future-frame from George Pal's *The Time Machine* three years later: Fungi people standing on various rocks in threatening poses. Even their body language says Morlock. What's more, Pete battles them with torches, just as Rod Taylor does in the later film.

I really like the surreal sight of a basement door (complete with window) in the underground cavern, looking somewhat like the elevator to hell. And there's a pleasing moment when Ramsey enjoys staring at Pete through the glass. When it's evident to the good doctor that the fungi, now exposed to the air, could take over the world, his suddenly panicky attitude seems just as ambiguous as the scientific laws governing the nature of this stuff (just what exactly does it do to people?). Ramsey then seems determined to destroy his own work, making us wonder if he is *more mad* or *less mad* than we thought.

Charles Marquis Warren (1912—1990) was an extremely diverse and interesting writer, director, and producer who, among other things, was instrumental in the development of both the *Gunsmoke* and *Rawhide* television series. *The Unknown Terror* and its quite different co-feature, *Back From the Dead* (the latter now on Film Masters Blu-ray, where I pipe in on Tom Weaver's commentary), were Warren's only forays into the fantastic. As a fan of both, I can only wish he'd done more.

The Woman Eater

1958

NADIA ROBERTSON

Although chided by some as the last breath of British quota quickies, the perversion portrayed in *The Woman Eater* makes it a movie worthy of appreciation for its sheer audacity. A title boasting pornographic suggestion already infringed on the status quo for acceptable Anglo-entertainment of its time. While America had already produced plenty of horror movies, England was still clutching its pearls trying to hold onto high-minded values through censorship of all things naughty and nasty. A puritanical system was put into practice that would seek to stifle creativity and control the salaciousness fans have come to love and expect from the genre: blood, boobs, and anything controversial that challenges the boring norms and played-out archetypes of the period.

The influx of American horror movies making their way overseas had prudes panicking enough to plea for a halt to the production of horror. A 16-and-older "X" Certificate was introduced in 1951 by the British Board of Film Classification and the label was slapped onto *The Woman Eater* upon its UK release through Eros Films in 1958. When Columbia Pictures distributed it in the US, like most other horror passing through the country, the movie was promoted as a children's picture, shown during Saturday matinees as if they were cartoons... because what mother wouldn't want to take her kiddies to a movie that sounds like it should be sequestered in the back room of some seedy video store. Horror was still struggling to be seen as serious, striving to be set free from its suppressive shackles, similarly to the women written within the story being controlled by their fictitious oppressors.

By the 1960's, interest started to shift into media more overt in its messages, pushing past subtlety that WE are the villains of the story, not some made-up monsters. Kids raised on drive-in movies were getting a taste for something more sinister, reflective of real life horrors they were experiencing around them. *The Woman Eater* pushed boundaries of the decade, though not quite satisfying the bloodthirst audiences were already developing after entertaining headier themes and allegory from the earlier era. The precarious black & white practical effects of the prop plant (which caught fire the first day filming, having to quickly be replaced) couldn't hold a candle to the colorful sensationalism Hammer Films offered with luscious-looking gore and vicious villains, especially considering that *The Curse of Frankenstein* came out the year before. Creative collaborators, director Charles Saunders and producer Guido Coen, sought a solution with *The Woman Eater* to adhere to code restrictions, while sneaking in sexual references and metaphors for misogyny during a time when women were being regulated on and off screen.

A plot predicated around sexual assault wouldn't necessarily call to mind a carnivorous plant, but *The Woman Eater* parallels the mayhem of flesh-eating foliage to mankind's mistreatment of females. The film focuses on a mad scientist, Dr. Moran, played by character actor, George Coulouris (*Citizen Kane*), whose motivations seem like old-fashioned B-movie fare with fantasies of fame for finding the secret to defeating death — a sadistic scientific experiment which requires sacrificing drugged double-D dames to JuJu, a jungle idol of the South American Incas. Feeding it only the most beautiful of buxom babes, Dr. Moran seeks to extract a serum formulated from the tree's sacred sap that resurrects the dead, and in turn, guarantees his own immortality through the glory gained from the groundbreaking discovery. There's no altruism for the betterment of mankind in his intent. He sees what he wants and takes it, assuming everything on Earth is for his exclusive benefit.

Upon locating the secluded tribe, Dr. Moran suffers 'jungle fever' in more ways than one. The trek to get there has built up such sweaty anticipation, he barely has the strength to carry on… until he comes across the ceremony, where he witnesses a drop-dead gorgeous local lady swaying to the beat of the tribal drums, a lurid act which reinvigorates his senses of seduction.

The wildly successful 1953 theatrical re-release of *King Kong* (1933) influenced some of history's greatest giant monster movies, including provocations of nudity, violence, and racial indiscretions which propagated white men's misguided presumptions of "wild savages", with *The Woman Eater* following suit, audaciously making no attempt to accurately portray its aboriginals (or Science, either — Dr. Moran's "Pulsometer" is charmingly simple), as if the attention to detail would be an afterthought to its purposely exploitative approach.

Juju's phallic plant appendages reach out to grasp the hottie it's hungry for, a la Alex in *A Clockwork Orange*, its outstretched vines conjuring Hentai-adjacent visuals of women entangled in titillated tentacles. The damsel in distress (the stunning Marpessa Dawn, starring a year later in *Black Orpheus*) snaps out of the spell, battling to break free, but the more she struggles, the more excited the groping greenery becomes to ravage her, coinciding with Dr. Moran's arousal as he watches the act against autonomy with Hitchcockian voyeurism, like some Peeping Tom prowler. A fellow explorer who has joined the demented doctor on his journey can't stand idly by as the innocent girl fights for her life, but a quick spear to the ribs reinforces the saying, "nice guys finish last," or in this case, die first.

Clashing with 1950's ideals of good girls and gentlemen coexisting in domestic bliss, the characters in *The Woman Eater* are more similar to antiheroes of film noir cinema, reflecting a change in morals that defined the decade leading up to the Sexual Revolution of the sixties and protests proving women have value beyond their bodies. Sally Norton, played by blonde bombshell, Vera Day (Britain's own Marilyn Monroe, known for modeling her torpedo bras), attracts customers at the circus by hula-dancing half-naked. Meanwhile, garage mechanic by day / white knight by night, Jack Venner (Peter Forbes-Robertson) falls in love with her at first sight but displays bouts of chauvinism. Though their budding relationship adds much character-driven charm to the story, they don't exactly fit the mold of proper people, even if attempting traditionalism by proposing marriage. Even during that sweet scene, the camera still centers its attention around her chest for clever laughs and meta-intended leering.

Dr. Moran's obsessions extend to Sally as he wishes to swap out his aging (and thusly used and useless) secretary / former lover for a newer model, as his quest for legacy spares no woman from exposure to his selfishness. His abusive cruelty equating her worth against her age drives her desire to choke the life out of the younger competition, just as the Juju squeezes the juices of youth from its victims. The contrasting couples parallel two different stages of a relationship: one budding and another wilting on the vine.

The Woman Eater pushed Britain's psychosexual boundaries of proprietary, and its basic premise would inspire other mad scientist and killer plant pictures in the following years, like *The Little Shop of Horrors* (1960, see later chapter) and *Konga* (1961, profiled in our previous book, *Giant Beast Cinema*). The film's most memorable sequence follows Dr. Moran as he stalks a randomly selected pedestrian as his next victim down the scuzzy streets of London whilst the prowling POV camera maneuvers through a real crowd — a creative choice in cinematography recalling Jack the Ripper and serving as a predecessor to the body-count sub-genres of Giallo and slasher-style horror with a similar urban sleaziness to that of Frank Henenlotter (*Basket Case*, *Frankenhooker*).

Consumers purchase highly sought-after products synthesized from exotic plants to extend the duration of their physical beauty. *The Woman Eater* warns that what women strive to maintain may be what society manipulates to gobble them up - depicting the misogynistic insight that if you're already middle-aged, then heck, you might as well be dead.

The Little Shop of Horrors

1960

PHOEF SUTTON

Mushnik's Florist shop will live forever.

Or at least it's been going strong for sixty-five years and shows no signs of losing its appeal. True, sometimes it's called *Mushnik's Flower Shop*, but brand names change over the years. Mushnik's is located on Skid Row, "where the tragedies are deeper, the ecstasies wilder, and crime rates consistently higher than anywhere else." That's how Charles B. Griffith put it in his classic screenplay for the film, *The Little Shop of Horrors*.

Little Shop is a film that defies all expectations. It's the blackest of black comedies, but somehow comes across as good-natured and light-hearted. It's filled with death, but somehow life affirming. It was made on a shoe-string budget, but has outlasted the biggest budgeted movies of its day.

The original *Little Shop* came out in 1960 and was a 'B' feature –

CINEMA BIZARRO

possibly a 'C' or 'D' feature, if the alphabet of movie labels went that low. The script was written in one weekend and filmed (under the direction of the great Roger Corman) in two or possibly three days. It was made this quickly because Corman wanted to beat a change in industry rules requiring residual payments to actors. It was shot with three cameras running simultaneously in the manner of a TV situation comedy. For budgetary reasons, most of the film takes place in one room (it isn't hard to imagine it as a play, as Alan Menken and Howard Ashman did in the 80s). All in all, it was just a quickie, made to fill out the double-bill at a local drive-in and then be forgotten. It was such a neglected film that its copyright was never renewed and it fell into Public Domain.

But, like the carnivorous plant, Audrey Jr., the movie seems to have a life and a mind of its own. It didn't make much of a splash when it was first released, but over time it became a cult movie, then the inspiration for an off-Broadway musical, then for a major motion picture. That the film has been revived and watched by millions of people, year after year, for over six decades would come as a total surprise to the people that made it. They were a talented group on the fringes of show business, just having the time of their lives and doing great work that they thought no one would pay any attention to. Most of them would have long careers in the industry and one member of the cast would become a major star. But they were all having fun, glad for the opportunity just to make a movie, never imagining one day, it would be considered a classic.

The story begins on Skid Row. To be specific, the outdoor locations were shot on the Skid Row of Los Angeles. It was called Bunker Hill and it's long gone, but in its heyday, it was the very incarnation of what we now call Film Noir. Hulking Victorian houses, crumbling storefront shops, and dark, foreboding railroad tracks.

The story is told to us by one Sgt. Joe Fink (Wally Campo). The fact that this narration is done in a parody of Jack Webb's *Dragnet* is no doubt lost on a 21st Century audience, but that probably just adds to the weird quirkiness of the film, starting with the black and white cartoon credits and percussive jazz score by Fred Katz.

We are soon introduced to Seymour Krelborn (Jonathan Haze) and Gravis Mushnik (Mel Welles). It is indicative of how slap-dash this production was that the spelling of the characters' names often varies from source to source. Mushnik owns the florist shop and Seymour is his hapless employee, emphasis on the hapless. Seymour is totally without hap. But that doesn't stop Seymour's co-worker Audrey Fulquard (Jackie Joseph) from doting on him in her scatterbrained fashion.

Seymour is clumsy and incompetent, but he does have one thing going for him: he is growing a very peculiar piece of flora that he names Audrey Jr. As customer Burson Fouch (the great Dick Miller) tells Mushnik, a flower shop that has an unusual plant will attract many customers.

But Seymour has a problem with Audrey Jr. The problem is that Audrey Jr. is a plant that thrives on only one thing. Human blood. And, as it grows, it gets more and more demanding. It even begins to speak. "Feed me!" it says (the voice is supplied by the uncredited Charles B. Griffith). And thus, Seymour is forced to go on an unwilling and unintentional killing spree.

There is also a subplot dealing with a sadistic dentist (John Herman Shaner) who delights in torturing his patients. While Seymour dispatches him as another meal for Audrey Jr., a masochistic patient shows up. This patient is Wilber Force and is played (with Jerry Lewis-syle mugging) by a young Jack Nicholson. Nicholson was just one of the great forces of 70s cinema that Roger Corman discovered or at least nurtured. Other Corman alumni include Martin Scorsese, Francis Ford Coppola, Peter Bogdanovich, James Cameron, Robert Towne, and the list goes on and on.

But Charles B. Griffith is the real creative genius behind *Little Shop of Horrors*. No disrespect to Roger Corman intended, but the genesis of the script came from Griffith, who played three parts in the film and directed the outdoor sequences which display the most cinematic flair of this mostly stage-bound film. Griffith's fingerprints are all over *The Little Shop of Horrors*.

Charles B. Griffith is one of the great unsung screenwriters of post-War American cinema. Of course, most screenwriters are unsung (quick, name one), but Griffith remained almost deliberately obscure. He had a voice as unique and poetic as Rod Serling or Paddy Chayefsky, but (perhaps because he didn't write for television like they did) he never rose to their heights. He never wrote an A-picture, although a lot of his pictures did make money.

Griffith mostly worked for Roger Corman because, he said, "I was lazy. Instead of trying to write an A-picture and sell it on the market, I'd just go back and get another assignment from Roger." His work includes the wonderful *A Bucket of Blood*, which served as something of a template for *The Little Shop of Horrors*.

His other films include *Gunslinger*, a progressive Western featuring a female sheriff (Beverly Garland), *Attack of the Crab Monsters* (another comic masterpiece), *Not of This Earth* (a terrifying film about an alien vampire), *The Undead, Creature From the Haunted Sea, The Wild Angels* (a motorcycle film which was a pre-cursor to Easy Rider), *Death Race 2000*, and *Eat My Dust* (which he also directed and was Roger Corman's most successful film of the 1970s).

His was one of the unique, humorous, and satiric voices of the 20th Century. With a few turns of fate, he could have been another Buck Henry or Terry Southern. As it is, he was Charles B. Griffith, and that should be enough for anybody.

In the Spring of 2024, I was lucky enough to attend a screening of *The Little Shop of Horrors* at the Philosophical Research Society in Los Feliz, California, hosted by the illustrious Justin Humphreys (who wrote five chapters for our previous book in this series, *Giant Beast Cinema*). In attendance was Jonathan Haze – Seymour Krelborn himself, one of the last surviving members the Little Shop team. To hear Jonathan and Justin talk after the screening was one of the highlights of my life.

As Audrey Jr. put it, "Feed me!"

The Day of the Triffids

1963

NADIA ROBERTSON

In elementary school, instead of listening to my science teacher's lessons, I was dedicated to doodling Audrey II, the menacing, man-eater antagonist from Frank Oz's 1986 film *The Little Shop of Horrors*. A childhood favorite watched relentlessly on repeat, the imaginative horror-comedy-musical made an everlasting impression on me, initiating an immediate interest in Venus Flytraps — a shared intrigue that must have been prevalent in the 90's zeitgeist, seeing as these curious oddities could be found for purchase in grocery stores back then. It wasn't until adulthood that I would later come across *The Day of the Triffids* to prompt a revisit to my fascination with flesh-eating flora. Surprisingly, what initially seemed a run-of-the-mill monster movie revealed a survivalist story reflecting the ravaged psyche of a war-worn England attempting to cope with the aftereffects of armed conflict.

The preposterous concept of meteor-shower-activated carnivorous plants in *The Day of the Triffids* (director, Steve Sekely) may seem innocuous compared to the more immediate threats at the time of the film's 1963 premiere. A science fiction story countering man against prowling shrubbery deceptively showcases itself as another in-vogue, low budget, creature feature. However, the peculiar plot harbors hidden themes, like the inconspicuous enemy lying in wait (titular Triffids) and presents an underlying, unexpected bleakness in a B-movie facade as an

CINEMA BIZARRO

analogue for WWII anxieties stemming from the country's vulnerability during the continual Cold War.

The Day of the Triffids sets up the illusion of safety with a seemingly harmless initial celestial situation leading to an all-too-deadly lesson in not letting one's guard down around an omnipresent opponent. The film begins after a spectacular shower of shooting stars punishes those people who peeked at the phenomenon by rendering them blind. To compound these catastrophic consequences, predatory plants uproot themselves to stalk people as prey. Thus, the earlier frenzied media reports, pressing people not to miss this "once in a lifetime" astronomical event, have inadvertently helped to exacerbate the problem, reflecting a real feeling of the then-current consciousness when war had not just been waged on the battlefield, but also by the news-making media by way of quickly spreading fear tactics, propaganda, and rampant misinformation. Surely, that couldn't happen today, could it?

The subsequent societal collapse caused by the effects of mass blindness leaves humanity exposed to hazards of all kinds, not limited to the aggressive galactic greenery, but also including ill-intended individuals taking advantage of the weak. A few people still possessing their eyesight, marooned merchant naval officer, Bill Masen (Howard Keel), sensitive orphan stowaway Susan (Janina Faye), and philanthropic French governess, Christine (Nicole Maurey) are thrown into a makeshift, newfound family through chaotic circumstances that forces them on the run through various countrysides, seeking refuge.

Complementing the perspective to the trio's agoraphobic misadventures is the claustrophobic relationship of a resentful, sea-bound scientist couple, Karen (Janette Scott) and Tom (Kieron Moore) Goodwin, whose metaphorical, rocky relationship is made literally "on the rocks" as they struggle, stranded in a lighthouse on an isolated island, a marital strain accentuated by a fight against alcoholism. Forced to abandon the bottle to band together and battle both man's self-destructive nature as well as the impeding plants, husband and wife must reignite their will to live to unveil the secret to their survival. This additional seaside storyline was incorporated after the studio's dissatisfaction with the initial cut of the film, resulting in asking the aid of uncredited director/cinematographer Freddie Francis to pad out an otherwise too short runtime by inserting an alternate, more uplifting conclusion — much to the chagrin of readers claiming the movie's varying version of the story does a disservice to the supposedly darker original source material.

Those familiar with John Wyndham's 1951 novel share a general consensus that this first film adaptation is not adequately faithful, accused by readers of omitting the biting sociopolitical satire that offered thought-provoking subversions within the context of the book. The on-screen credit lists Executive Producer Philip Yordan as the seasoned screenwriter who tackled the adaptation. Yordan was a celebrated, veteran writer/producer of many classic film noirs and had just come off the 1961 epics, *King of Kings* and *El Cid*. Yordan, however, was fronting for the actual uncredited screenwriter, his friend Bernard Gordon, who was blacklisted by the House on Un-American Activities. Perhaps when this elusive film is finally released on DVD or BluRay, the correct writing credit will be restored, as it has been for many films of this period.

Operating under the guise of a standard "end of the world" melodrama, what *The Day of the Triffids* truly captures is an atmosphere of chaos triggered by the abrupt interruption of a recently reestablished new world order following WWII. The widely-varied human responses to the decay of civilization is made to be as frightening as the man-eating monsters. Although audiences deem the film's finale as too simple a solution to such a devastating problem, the lingering implication of society's possibly permanent dissolution still hangs decidedly unresolved. A wartime-ravaged audience might prefer a conveniently cathartic resolution in lieu of facing the harsh facts of reality, but the residual effects of mass-scale destruction are not to be easily dismissed.

Not so seamless SFX may be a reminder that B-movies function off minimal financing, relying on the viewer's imagination to compensate for imperfect practical effects. The Triffids pictured on the posters promise better designs than what was delivered, but still effectively evoke dread. While *The Day of the Triffids* falls into the limitations of a low budget production, the film's eerie tone elevates it from being a forgettable entry in the "violent vegetation" sub-genre. Switching from a creepy orchestral accompaniment to an absence of score, the minimal use of music maximizes the tension amplified in ambience to either echo silence (where there should be everyday, bustling soundscape) or to sustain anxiety amongst sudden screams echoing in an alarming apocalyptic aftermath.

Notable influence from *The Day of the Triffids* has since been attributed to iconic moments in popular modern horror movies and TV, including both opening sequences to Danny Boyle's *28 Days Later* and the *The Walking Dead* pilot episode, reenacting waking to a discombobulated state of disarray with no means of discerning the direness of the looming danger. The allusion to an overwhelming necessity to adapt or otherwise perish shares the paralyzing challenges presented by recovering from the trauma of a recently decimated infrastructure.

Despite the film adaptation truncating the novel's themes, the allegories to Cold War commentary following England's reconstruction after the Second World War retain focus on the disastrous outcome of being unprepared against a concealed combatant, culminating in civil unrest similar to the mania brewing under the veil of Russia's Iron Curtain. Perhaps the movie's deus ex machina conclusion mirrors both the characters' and the audience's long awaited reward for adhering to the praised "pull yourself up by your bootstraps", proactive approach of nationalistic-driven England attempting to rally dulled morale during its post-war rebuilding.

Regardless of comparisons to the book, the silver screen adaptation of *The Day of The Triffids* manages to balance some unanticipated humor to undercut its suspense, alleviating otherwise darker themes of humanity's dual existence in a world without moral absolutes. An alternative twist to an ambiguous end sends movie viewers home with a hopeful outlook on humanity's perseverance amongst any kind of opposition, fictitious or not.

Despite decades dedicated to producing a proper, pristine version, film restoration expert Mike Hyatt's posthumous dream project has yet to come to pass. One can hold out hope that such a noble aspiration will become a reality for wishful cinephiles… unlike the possibility of plants becoming hungry for humans.

MATANGO

1963/1965

BRIAN R. SOLOMON

Although one of the lesser-known films of Japanese science fiction master Ishiro Honda, thanks mainly to the vagaries of international film distribution, *Matango* (also known in the United States and Canada as *Attack of the Mushroom People*) also happens to be one of his very best. A moody, dark piece that's part body horror and part tense psychodrama, it is unique among the copious output of *tokusatsu* ("special effects") and *kaiju* flicks churned out by Toho and other Japanese film studios during the country's science fiction boom of the late 1950's and 1960's. Despite the fact that it never got a proper stateside theatrical release at the time, it was one of those genre films that found its home on late night television, and was reappraised thanks to niche home video distributors much later on. That's a good thing, because it would have been a shame if this gem had been consigned to the void of cinema oblivion.

Based in part on the 1907 short story "The Voice in the Night" by William Hope Hodgson, first published in the vaunted sci-fi pulp magazine *Blue Book*, as well as a later story by Shinichi Hoshi that had appeared in Japan's *S-F Magazine*, the film tells the tale of a group of pleasure-cruising young people who find themselves shipwrecked on an island in the grip of a strange, predatory fungus that possesses and consumes them all, one by one. There are hints here of *Invasion of the Body Snatchers* (1956, reviewed in an earlier chapter) for sure, and it's also clear that John Carpenter had to have seen this picture before mounting his 1982 remake of *The Thing*, which mimics much of *Matango*'s pervasive paranoia and claustrophobia. And like Carpenter's film, it is played completely straight, with a dramatic edge that Honda reportedly encouraged, sensing that the film should be a bit more of a prestige drama than most of his genre output was known for being.

The cast that Toho and executive producer Tomoyuki Tanaka assembled to pull this off is quite the impressive one, boasting some of the studio's most polished and proven players. The youthful Akira Kubo, who had worked with Honda just the year before on *Gorath*, as well as with none other than Akira Kurosawa on *Throne of Blood* (1957), plays the desperate Prof. Kenji Murai, sole survivor of the film's events, whose recollections form the main flashback plot. Honda and Kubo's relationship would continue with *Invasion of Astro-Monster* (1965), *Son of Godzilla* (1967), *Destroy All Monsters* (1968) and *Space Amoeba* (1970). The beautiful Kumi Mizuno, best known as Miss Namikawa alongside Nick Adams in *Invasion of Astro-Monster*, plays glamorous singer Mami Sekiguchi, who ultimately turns treacherous when she begins to take pleasure in the shipwrecked men fighting over her. She later gives in to the influence of the mushrooms, leading into the movie's taut climax, in which she lures Murai directly into the heart of the fungal infestation.

There's omnipresent Toho and *tokusatsu* veteran Kenji Sahara, who distinguishes himself as ship's first mate Senzo Koyama, assistant to ship's captain Naoyuki Sakuda, played by a brooding Hiroshi Koizumi of *Godzilla Raids Again* (1955) and *Mothra* (1961) fame. Even Yoshio Tsuchiya, one of Kurosawa's favorite players, turns up as cynical industrialist Masafumi Kasai, the owner of the vessel, who cordons himself off from the rest of the passengers and begins hoarding supplies as soon as the situation begins to grow dire.

It all plays on a much more cerebral level than much of the other genre fare coming out of Japan (or anywhere, for that matter) at the time. These are all clearly characters with backstories we are only partially privy to, with relationships that inform their actions. In short, they have an internal life we don't often get to see in movies of this nature. The script crackles along, and is one of the very best ever produced by frequent Honda collaborator Takeshi Kimura. As with all great horror movies, it builds tension expertly, and is much more about what you don't see than what you do.

It's all complemented by the muted colors and stark production design work of Shigekazu Ikuno. And of course, there is the always-imaginative special effects of Toho's legendary effects head Eiji Tsuburaya, joined by his first assistant Teruyoshi Nakano, who would later take over the division after Tsuburaya took ill in the late 1960's. Both men brought monsters like Godzilla, Mothra and Rodan to life in other films, but this movie affords them a chance to do things a little differently.

Honda was a thoughtful and skilled filmmaker who had made a living in the Japanese film industry for years before *Gojira* (1954) changed the course of his career forever. By the end of the decade, for better or worse, he'd be saddled almost entirely with science-fiction, horror, and fantasy, and *Matango* was in fact his 13th film in this vein. But it was the fact that his sensibilities as a filmmaker had been honed on more "serious" pictures, often at the side of his great friend Kurosawa, that allowed Honda to bring so much to the genre pictures he'd tackle in the last 10-15 years of his fully active career. He saw them as much more than simple popcorn fare, and *Matango* is a great example of this attitude, with its themes of social isolation, existential threats to Japan's cultural identity through Western influences, and of course, the dangers of nuclear experimentation—a common touchstone in many Japanese science-fiction films of the period. In fact, in the film, the mutations of the island's natural fungal life into dangerous, parasitic spores is chalked up directly to the atomic testing that the United States had been doing in the South Pacific in the years after World War II.

When the film was released in Japan in August 1963, there were some moves to ban it, due to the depiction of victims whose faces eerily

CINEMA BIZARRO

resembled those who'd suffered radiation burns from the real-life atomic bombings of Hiroshima and Nagasaki just 18 years prior. It was also a tough sell in the usually receptive North American market, due perhaps to its more subtle, psychological nature, the fact that it didn't have a giant monster, and that the titular "mushroom people" don't really show up in all their proto-psychedelic glory until the end. It did find its way to television in 1965 thanks to the efforts of Samuel Z. Arkoff and James H. Nicholson at American International Pictures (AIP).

Although it would never be seen on the big screen, *Matango* made a huge impression among future filmmakers like Guillermo del Toro and Steven Soderbergh, who caught it on late night TV and never forgot it. It disappeared again in the age of home video, but was given the deluxe treatment on DVD and Blu Ray in the 2000's by boutique houses like Media Blasters and Tokyo Shock, bringing it to new generations of film lovers in the English-speaking world. Soderbergh even once attempted to mount an American remake of the film, but Toho's notoriously tough rights negotiations wound up nixing the project.

For those seeking a more subtle take on Japanese monster horror, that's part *Alien* and part *Ten Little Indians*, look no further than *Matango*, the thinking person's radioactive fungus movie. Come for the humanoid polyurethane mushroom costumes, stay for the locked-room melodrama.

Die Monster Die!

1965

PHOEF SUTTON

When I was growing up, I wasn't just a Monster Kid. I was also a Lovecraft fan, or a Cthulhu Mythos Maniac, as no one but me ever called them. I used to sit in my room and devour the Ballantine paperback editions (with the brilliant John Holmes cover art) of *The Lurking Fear*, *At the Mountains of Madness*, *The Tomb*, and all the others. In my mind, I visited Arkham and Innsmouth and Dunwich, and audited classes at Miskatonic University.

This was long before the days of the mass acceptance of H.P. Lovecraft as one of the premiere writers of American Literature and weird fiction. Before the days of the *Call of Cthulhu* role-playing game and cuddly, stuffed Cthulhu-teddy-bears. In those days, I thought I was pretty much alone in my adulation of all things Lovecraftian. My use of words like "eldritch" and "noisome" and the ever-popular "bachtrachian" elicited nothing more than blank stares from my classmates. I never thought I'd live to see the Library of American publish a volume of Lovecraft tales. Now, I have seen this and more.

As far as film adaptations, by the mid-1960's, there had only been one H. P. Lovecraft tale turned into a movie. Disguised as an American International Pictures Edgar Allan Poe film, *The Haunted Palace* (1963) was an adaptation by *Twilight Zone* alumnus Charles Beaumont of Lovecraft's classic tale, "The Case of Charles Dexter Ward" starring Vincent Price. Before that, the only media adaptation that I'm aware of is a wonderful version of "The Dunwich Horror" done for the radio series *Suspense*, first broadcast in 1945 and starring Ronald Colman, of all people. (You can find it on YouTube and it's well worth a half-hour of your time.)

The next Lovecraft film adaptation came out in 1965, also produced by American International, and was based on his classic short story "The Colour Out of Space" (note the British-style spelling of "color;" Lovecraft was an unrelenting Anglophile). Filmed under the evocative title *The House at the End of the World* but released under the more schlocky monikers, *Die, Monster, Die!* in the U.S. and *Monster of Terror* in the U.K, this movie was an awkward hybrid of the Cthulhu Mythos and a Roger Corman/Poe picture.

The screenplay is by Jerry Sohl. Like the aforementioned Charles Beaumont, Sohl was a member of the Southern California group of speculative fiction writers nicknamed "The Green Hand." Beaumont was the lively leader of the group, which included Richard Matheson, William F. Nolan, George Clayton Johnson, Robert Bloch, and Ray Bradbury. They talked, networked, drank, and wrote for *The Twilight Zone*, *Playboy* magazine, the Roger Corman films, and various pulp publications. Famously, Jerry Sohl began to ghost-write for Beaumont when he began to show symptoms of the illness that finally took his life – most notably, the terrifying *Twilight Zone* featuring Talky Tina: "Living Doll." Beaumont suffered from a combination of Alzheimer's disease and Pick's disease, which caused him to age quickly and devastatingly. He died at age thirty-eight, but according to his son, he looked like a man of ninety-five. Beaumont was suffering from this terrible fate while Sohl was writing the screenplay. This tragedy casts a melancholy shadow over *Die, Monster, Die!*

The film begins with Stephen Reinhart (played by Nick Adams, an actor who, as my daughter puts it, "has a face you just want to slap") arriving by train at the British village of Arkham (That's right, Lovecraft's

DIE, MONSTER, DIE!

Arkham has been transplanted from Massachusetts to England, just one of the many changes from the source material.) Here, Stephen is faced with what may be called "the Jonathan Harker greeting" – no sooner does he say that he wants to go to "the Witley place" than everyone turns away from him and offers him no transport. He can't even rent a bicycle, for goodness' sake.

As Stephen takes the long walk to the Witley place, he passes a massive crater and an area of withered, blackened vegetation. This is what Lovecraft calls "the blasted heath" and sets the viewer up for a chilling adventure. It's a promise that will only partly be fulfilled.

When Stephen reaches his destination, the film borrows many elements from the Corman/Vincent Price films. The Witley house is a grand, decaying mansion, far from the humble farmhouse of the Lovecraft story. Stephen (a character invented for the movie) is there to visit his girlfriend, Susan (also invented for the movie, played by Suzan Farmer, who would star in two Hammer Films the very next year: *Dracula: Prince of Darkness* and *Rasputin: the Mad Monk*), but is greeted coldly by her father, Nahum Witley (Boris Karloff), who tells him to leave. Karloff is taking the Vincent Price role here, but approaching eighty, and in a wheelchair, he cuts a more dignified and poignant figure than Price usually did.

Stephen refuses to leave and he and Susan try to understand the many mysteries of the house. For one thing, there's Susan's mother, Letitia (Freda Jackson), suffering from a baffling ailment and keeping herself hidden, shrouded in a fourposter bed. For another, there's the strange, glowing stone Nahum keeps in a well in the basement. And then, when Stephen and Susan are examining the strange vegetation in the greenhouse, they took a look at the potting shed and there they find a set of horribly deformed mutations locked in cages.

"It's like a zoo in hell," Stephen says.

Then Susan almost gets eaten by one of the plants in the greenhouse. This scene is one of the film's high points.

In the end, Letitia mutates into a full-blown monster and Nahum reveals that the glowing stone was a meteor that fell to earth and made the vegetation grow lush. Nahum took the fragments of the meteorite back to the house to study it before he knew the full horror of its cosmic

CINEMA BIZARRO

radiation. Now, Nahum changes his tune and begs Stephen to take Susan away with him. But, of course, Nahum himself is transformed into a mutant as he tries to destroy the meteor. Nahum (now a glowing stunt man) tries to kill Stephen and Susan, only to fall off the landing of the great house and burst into flame. Then Stephen and Susan walk off, with Stephen explaining where Nahum went wrong.

"The Colour Out of Space" has been adapted to film surprisingly often. After *Die, Monster, Die!*, there was *The Curse* (1987), *Colour From the Dark* (2008), *The Colour Out of Space* (*Die Farbe*) (2010) and *Color Out of Space* (2019). I confess, I've only seen the last of these subsequent versions. Directed by Richard Stanley and starring Nicolas Cage, it is far more faithful (in spirit at least) to the Lovecraft original. It is highly recommended.

Die, Monster, Die! is not a great film, mostly due to the performance of Nick Adams, as a hero who seems to be "mansplaining" even when he's just listening. However, it does have much going for it. Mostly, the heartbreaking portrayal of Nahum Witley by Boris Karloff, but also Freda Jackson's eerie performance as Letitia. And of course, the hideous and yet strangely cute mutations from "the zoo in hell."

All in all, this is promising directorial debut by art director Daniel Haller. As art director, Haller was responsible for Roger Corman's *House of Usher*, *The Pit and the Pendulum*, and *The Masque of the Red Death*. As director, he went on to do *The Dunwich Horror* and a slew of network television episodes, including *Night Gallery* and *Kojak*. He's still with us, raising horses on his ranch in the San Fernando Valley.

As far as I know, no meteor has fallen on his ranch.

Dr. Terror's House of Horrors

1965

NADIA ROBERTSON

Anthologies employ a built-in formula for pleasing general audiences by offering a sample platter of plots bundled within a feature length film without fully committing to a singular story that may not sustain mass appeal. Historically, horror has flourished in the short story form and Amicus Productions parlayed the versatility of the vignette structure into a prosperous template for producing a revered repertoire of paranormal portmanteau films responsible for pioneering the company's commercial and creative peak during the trajectory of Britain's gothic decade burgeoning between the 1960's through the 1970's.

Staking a claim to contemporary pieces as a signature counterpoint to Hammer Films' compendium of period commodities (*Frankenstein*, *Dracula*, *The Mummy*, et al), Amicus' founding fathers, Milton Subotsky and Max Rosenberg, siphoned from the same pool of onscreen performers and behind-the-camera creatives to build their own roster of talent, a cost-effective strategy against their better known competitor. Establishing a foundation erected from scavenged creative components may have tapped into Amicus' subconscious sensitivity to any allegations of being a lesser version of its influences, though an impression of self-awareness from the studio could point to accepting the similarities motivated from the muses seen in Subotsky's writing.

Following *The Twilight Zone* series finale the year before and the general popularity of E.C. Comics' episodic stories, the briskly-paced supernatural format garnered attention from studios cashing in on the lucrative narrative structure, attracting audiences looking for a variety of scares served up in one package with a surprise twist. Subotsky's avid adoration of the macabre proposed a tonal blueprint for Amicus' first anthology horror film, *Dr. Terror's House of Horrors* (1965), a five-part script inspired by *Dead of Night* (1945) from Ealing Studios, a successful anthology he admired and sought to emulate by following a similar structure within his own filmography.

Ultimately, and despite the studio's efforts to the contrary, *Dr. Terror*'s triggered Amicus's unfair reputation as a pale imitator to Hammer Films, which were scoring international success with their colorfully garish gothic horrors. However, unlike Hammer, which often had a head start with the financial support of major American studios, Amicus couldn't convince Columbia Pictures to finance a coproduction.

The setback didn't stop Amicus from laying the groundwork for success by hiring from Hammer's rolodex of royalty, bringing aboard Britain's horror poster boys, Peter Cushing and Christopher Lee, cast next to charismatic costars (including Michael Gough and American newcomer, Donald Sutherland). To service the story's polished visual panache, Amicus also brought on Oscar-winning cinematographer, Freddie Francis (who had just directed three Hammer films in a row) to direct, alongside the sharp eye of Alan Hume (*Lifeforce*, *Return of the Jedi*) as the film's Director of Photography. *Dr. Terror's House of Horrors*' Technicolor-treated color palette lusciously paints a lively picture, permeating a vibrant energy enhanced by lavish-looking sets built on Shepperton Studios' soundstages, consciously designed to complement Amicus' aspiring creative ambitions within the restrictions of the company's minimal monetary means.

The advent of Amicus' anthological framework facilitated an innovative bookending narrative style soon to become the company's calling card. The film centers around five unsuspecting passengers sharing a compartment as they travel by train with Dr. Sandor Schreck (Cushing), whose name translating to "Terror" recalls lead actor, Max Schreck, in 1922's silent classic, *Nosferatu*. Dr. Schreck is a demonic creature claiming victims under the guise of an unassuming man, a mysterious "Scholar of Metaphysics". During their introduction, Schreck's deck of prophetic tarot cards "conveniently" spills into sight, deemed his

DR. TERROR'S HOUSE OF HORRORS

eponymous "House of Horrors". Capturing the curiosity of his fellow travelers, he proceeds to read their fortunes, reluctantly revealing a pre-destined fate, to each one's dismay. The ironic caveat to their enigmatic end suggest death as an alternate route to salvation, dodging otherwise obscure outcomes - perhaps an allusion to the uncertain future of the protagonists, as well as a more literal assessment of the startup studio's ability to survive.

The concepts Amicus built their budding business model upon could warrant accusations of recycling tired tropes well-worn past their prime. Uninspired segment titles ("Werewolf", "Creeping Vine", "Voodoo", "Disembodied Hand" and "Vampire") attempt to cover the spread of typical archetypes. But one of the film's scrappy strengths is blending classic themes with subtextual self-reflection beyond just rehashing B-movies' "Greatest Horror Hits".

As foreseen through Dr. Terror's tarot: Jim Dawson (Neil McCallum) is summoned to renovate his ancestral estate, now occupied by a new owner harboring intent to implement a sinister scheme scheduled on the next lunar cycle. Bill Rogers (DJ Alan Freeman) returns home to discover horticulture has become a hostile hobby on his homestead. Rising jazz musician, Biff Bailey (entertainer Roy Castle), reaps the voodoo wrath of cultural appropriation and copyright infringement. Contrarian critic Franklyn Marsh (Lee) learns a lesson regarding revenge as a repercussion for humoring artistic arrogance. And lastly, Dr. Bob Caroll (Sutherland) suffers great loss from gaslighting as bystander to a battle between bloodsuckers.

Examining the fledging studio's mindset may suggest self-referential sentiments coinciding with the cautionary assessments of all five of Dr. Terror's readings, subverting the meta-textual context of competing against Hammer Horror. For example, intruding on a dynastic, driven contender -- like Jim Dawson inadvertently does -- could mirror Amicus Productions' wariness of going up against a studio that had already strongly made their mark on the UK market, as well as preemptively jumping on judgements against skulking in the shadows of their predecessor's prosperity by plotting a takeover of their territory.

Sculpting a story about fast-adapting vines seeking to plant roots on private property also demonstrates an evolution towards acquisition

CINEMA BIZARRO

aimed at self-preservation, which could also be said for the studio creeping in on Hammer's talent as a survival tactic.

Plagiarism plagues Biff Bailey, as he models his music from mooched material, reflecting a shared attraction to the occult with the story's author and showcasing a cheeky attitude toward the consequences of copying from powerful, pre-established entities.

Franklin Marsh's relentless skepticism represents a scathing critique of art criticism, calling out critics for spitting snobbery at horror as an inherently "lesser" genre, slighting companies like Amicus who embraced its elements despite any possible pompous reception.

And finally, Dr. Bob Carroll's self-destructive decisions cost him when competition from a colleague decimates a dream of domestic bliss, signaling symbolism for rivalry sported against Amicus from the start. Even the stylish "wrap around" sequences serve as an analogy for the studio forging an ambiguous path through the frightening unknown, an incalculable, final destination leading to either fortune or death by defeat.

Although comparisons would be made for years between Hammer and Amicus as pillars of the British horror industry, limitations did not hinder the underdog company from concocting its own niche market to establish an enduring legacy. The success of *Dr. Terror's House of Horrors* stands testament to the triumph of the film's star power, its visually impactful compositions, and the creator's love of the genre - all distinguishing ingredients which, when combined, result in an atmospheric smorgasbord of supernatural stories to savor, showing the Sixties scene that Amicus was born ready to run with the big dogs.

By working with what resources they had, taking ownership of their trademarks, and setting the stage for many modern movies to draw from its influence, *Dr. Terror's House of Horrors* shows that whether Amicus was considered a champion or a charlatan, charmingly, it turns out that imitation may indeed be the sincerest form of flattery.

THE NAVY VS THE NIGHT MONSTERS

1966

TRACY MERCER

One might think that with a title like *The Navy vs. the Night Monsters*, this 1966 creature feature would have a vast cinematic scope, be loaded with hordes of terrifying creatures and feature a dazzling climax that displays the massive power of US military might! Well… you may want to readjust your expectations. Instead, you should know that this independent film (which is also known to fans under the titles, *Monsters of the Night* and *The Night Crawlers*) is a rather standard but still entertaining schlocky exercise. It is probably best remembered for the casting of blonde bombshell Mamie Van Doren as a nurse who wears form-fitting clothing as she assists a group of Navy men to vanquish… KILLER PLANTS!

CINEMA BIZARRO

The Navy vs. the Night Monsters is adapted from the Murray Leinster 1959 novel, *The Monster from Earth's End*. British director Michael A. Hoey (son of Dennis Hoey, who played Inspector Lestrade in Universal's Sherlock Holmes film series) delivered a tight, 71-minute film that he maintained would have played better for audiences at that length. However, with the emergence of TV and the profits to be made with ancillary sales of films to the medium, the need for a film that was closer to an hour and a half necessitated reshoots. Executive producer Jack Broder (along with an uncredited Roger Corman) decided to maximize their investment and commissioned a more TV-friendly cut by hiring director Arthur C. Pierce (*Women of the Prehistoric Planet*) to shoot additional footage. This additional footage did add runtime, but the extra minutes also account for the film's uneven pacing and several scenes that are set in a mainland military base which ultimately pull focus from the main tension on Gow Island. Also, the cheaply lit and clearly soundstage-bound sets are in no way a convincing substitute for a real jungle.

I would be remiss if I didn't mention that *Night Monsters* also has one of my favorite creature movie tropes (a trope that we also discuss in the chapter on *The Creeping Terror*) where actors are forced to scream and stand still or just lay down so that a very slow moving and not scary monster can consume them. Kudos to the actors in this film who walk into moving trees and attempt to wrestle with fake branches! Still, the often unintentionally laughable dialogue and wooden acting by most of the actors involved do make for an enjoyably camptastic and retro night at the movies.

The film opens aboard an Air Force plane that is approaching a Navy weather station/refueling location on the South Pacific island of Gow. We learn that this plane is transporting a cargo of specimens (including prehistoric plants and penguins!) found during a recent scientific Antarctic expedition. Insipid banter between our two pilots about the quality of inflight sandwiches is abruptly broken up by strange movements in the cargo hold that are so strong the whole plane shakes. Mayhem quickly ensues as some unseen threat terrifies a crewman so badly, he jumps out of the plane. Screams and gunshots are heard! Before we know it, the plane crashes on the Gow Island runway, making it unusable for any planes to take off while also managing to destroy the island's only two-way radio and control tower.

The crashed plane effectively cuts our Navy station staff off from the rest of the world – but even bigger trouble lies ahead. It seems all the expedition scientists and the crew except for one pilot have disappeared from the wreckage. The lone surviving pilot can't reveal what happened as he's in such a state of shock, he is unable to speak (Although later, he will break out of his hospital bed and attack a few people on the base with no plot payoff.).

While the Navy station brass, lead by Lt. Brown (handsome Anthony Eisley) seeks answers for what exactly happened at 30,000 feet, the Navy's Dr. Beecham (Walter Sande) suggests planting the prehistoric Antarctic trees on the island would be a smart way to keep them alive for scientific study. It's probably best as a viewer not to think about the logic of taking trees that evolutionarily have lived in the Antarctic permafrost being able to flourish once planted in the soil of a South Pacific island.

Faster than you can say 'deus ex machina,' a huge tropical storm wreaks havoc on the island, and this weather event may have somehow triggered something in the freshly planted prehistoric trees. These ancient plants now appear to be secreting some kind of toxic/acidic residue. Modern viewers may wonder if the makers of *Alien* (1979) saw this film and if it had any influence on that film's face-hugger and xenomorphs having concentrated acid for blood? As with the xenomorphs, this film showcases the corrosive ooze from the 'monster' burning the skin of those who come too close to their proximity. Shoutout for the icky, gross "burn" makeup effects that only seem to be shown on male victims and not on the bare shoulder of a female character who gets splattered with the noxious goo.

Back to the story: Post-storm and still cut off from the outside world, our Navy men consult with their base doctor to figure out what is going on and how to best battle the nefarious monsters that are killing people on the base. After our doctor analyzes the acidic residue, it becomes clear that the prehistoric trees are now secreting liquid death as part of their biology, which has also transformed them into carnivorous monsters. Even worse – at night, these killer trees traverse the island! In one of the better kills seen on screen, a hapless Navy guy walks into one of these trees and has his arm ripped off (sans any blood) for his efforts. These murderous trees appear to be able to reproduce and multiply quickly, thus threatening the lives of all on the base. Homemade Molotov cocktails prove to be effective in burning up the trees and now our navy team has a strategy to defeat the tree menace! Fire!

A little ingenuity, tied to the reality that the film needs an ending, means that our Navy boys are able to fix their two-way radio and restore contact with the outside world. They call in the cavalry (in this case, the cavalry appears to be stock footage of a handful of Blue Angels in flight, combined with stock footage of napalm being dropped on island locations). Amazingly, our surviving human characters live to see another day and we are left with a hint that a thinly-mentioned love story between Van Doren's nurse and Eisley's Lt. can now happen. The climax of fire and brimstone and smoldering stock footage is sold under a knee slapper of a summary: "Gow Island, in the past, virtually unknown to the rest of the word, today is a famous landmark in man's struggle with the unknown and another step forward in the march for science!" The ending seems to imply we had to destroy the island to save the island.

While certainly silly and ultimately not memorable, *The Navy vs. the Night Monsters* is an entertaining enough diversion that for many science fiction fans will likely play like a cheeky variant on *The Thing from Another World* (1951, see earlier chapter). After all, both films are centered on a group of people cut off from society, dealing with a nefarious force that has ties to killer-plants dug up from permafrost. But that's where the similarities end as no one will confuse this clunkily fun flick with that 1951 landmark classic film.

VENUS FLYTRAP

(aka, The Revenge of Doctor X, Body of the Prey)

1966/1970

MARK BAILEY

Venus Flytrap is a charming mess of a low-budget horror/sci-fi film with loads of entertainment value. A public domain movie, it was written, directed, and produced by Norman Earl Thompson and largely made overseas in Japan. I found the film enjoyable within the context of what it was, a second-rate genre movie with a cool, albeit clumsy, plant monster. Let me explain.

The story opens in what looks to be an incredibly drab 1960's office at Cape Canaveral during the very tense days leading up to a NASA launch. Here, we see our lead character, Dr. Bragan, grow more frustrated over unfavorable updates from his assistant about the looming deadline. Dr. Bragan is played by the aging, yet charming and capable James Craig and his John Waters-esque pencil-thin mustache (I would love to see Divine [Harris Glenn Milstead] deal with a plant monster, but I digress). Dr. Paul Nakamura, the assistant delivering the bad news, is played by James Yagi, who some may remember from his brief role in *King Kong vs. Godzilla* (1962).

After the successful launch, our hero is presented with newly-discovered "mathematical errors" that could potentially jeopardize long-term results of the NASA mission's success, and he then has a breakdown due to his nonstop schedule and years of work-related stress. After giving him a hard drink and encouraging some reflection, Dr. Nakamura suggests that Dr. Bragan take a long break in his home country of Japan where he can relax and embrace his first scientific interest in botany.

The musical score for this film can get very schmaltzy, and the departure scene of Dr. Bragan from Florida is no exception. The xylophone and organ accompaniment remind me of a time that never existed, a mix of late 60's Elks Lodge Dance Mixers and a long-deceased relative being remembered at a funeral home.

Car trouble forces the good doctor to pull over at a service station where a very colorful owner encourages him to look around his roadside zoo while his car gets fixed. This is where the title character is first introduced in the form of a small, potted Venus flytrap. Bragan is so enamored with the bizarre plant that he decides to go out and dig up one of his own in the nearby brush. With the titular plant safely stored in a small protective box and his car repaired, Bragan completes his drive to the airport.

Upon landing in Japan, Dr. Bragan is met by Noriko Hanamura (cousin of his assistant Dr. Paul Nakamura), played by the comely Atsuko Rome. Discovering that Miss Hanamura comes from a family that owns a number of resort hotels, it's decided that Dr. Bragan should recuperate in one of their more remote locations.

While driving a fun convertible to the doctor's scientific retreat, a very cheap-looking landslide forces them to pull over, where they witness an equally wonky volcanic eruption. This particular volcano special effect is a composite shot of a real mountain superimposed over footage of a mediocre explosion, and the resulting visual is unconvincing to modern audiences (and, I suspect, those in 1966). But I feel the filmmakers earned a bit more credibility with this somewhat childish looking volcano, given they could've just used stock footage.

More music ushers the couple on their continued drive and they reach the dilapidated resort. Here they meet the Quasimodo-like caretaker who can play Bach's *Toccata & Fugue in D Minor* on a pipe organ. Once settled into the hotel's greenhouse, Dr. Bragan sets out to commit his recreational mad science. During a break on their travels and research, Dr. Bragan speaks of his hope to graft his Venus flytrap to a venus vesiculosa (aka: aldrovanda vesiculosa, a carnivorous marine plant) and make an even more fierce and hearty botanical specimen. They decide to take a quick detour to the very picturesque Chiba Coast of Japan, where they hope to find the second specimen/ingredient to this leafy cocktail, a living venus vesiculosa.

This portion of the film features some female divers and brief, full frontal nudity – strange for a film with very little blood, mostly implied violence, and no harsh language. The scene is not salacious nor raunchy, but more like how *National Geographic* handles images of barely clothed indigenous peoples. This is a place where the filmmakers went the extra mile and shot underwater footage of the searching scientists and divers. I was again impressed that they did so when they could've used stock footage.

The scientists and local divers finally emerge on the beach with the rather rubbery-looking plant, package it, and get it back to the lab. A lab-work montage shows the scientists growing ever closer to merging the two carnivorous plants. This is supported with comically large plant specimens as well as an increasing amount of Flash Gordon movie serial era scientific equipment. All of this finally culminates with a lightning storm, beeping lab apparatuses, and throbbing pulses of animated electricity that bring our titular creature to life. The unveiling of the monster to the audience starts low on the creature's menacing feet (they have fangs) and slowly crawls up to reveal the enormous, hideous botanical fever dream in all its unnatural glory. Though the monster uses brilliantly red Venus flytrap hands that look like a cross between boxing gloves and baseball mitts, overall, it's pretty good, considering the budget. In fact, no plant monster this fascinating would come from Japan until the immensely entertaining *Godzilla vs. Biollante* (1989).

Upon consuming an unlucky puppy that wanders too close to the creature's deadly appendages, it's obvious that the monster has an appetite for flesh and blood. Dr. Bragan succumbs to his growing mania, ordering that more animals be fed to the monster, and then goes on to bleed a patient at a nearby sanitorium to add to the nourishing carnage.

A Frankenstein-inspired lightning storm brings us back to the lab, where the creature has devoured a guard dog. This is one of the more effective scenes, where the creature shows us the dog's collar and chain dangling from one of its deadly, flytrap hands.

Dr. Bragan decides to watch the creature, hoping to witness its independent movement, only to have it release some kind of tranquilizing mist. Once the doctor and his assistant are fast asleep, the monster literally uproots itself and goes on a murderous walkabout through a nearby village. In another nod to *Frankenstein*, we get the innocent deaths of a playful child and donkey cart driver, as well as vengeful, torch-bearing villagers seeking to destroy the monster. Dr. Bragan ultimately confronts his creation, and both meet their doom by falling into stock footage of flowing lava.

Crypto-filmographers have zealously heralded this film as derived from an Edward D. Wood Jr. (*Plan 9 From Outer Space*) script, but there is very little data documenting the actual production to support any such claims. In the numerous media I've consumed about Ed Wood, I've never heard of this film nor confirmed his alleged involvement. *Venus Flytrap* doesn't feel like an Ed Wood script; it has no long-winded speeches or mind-boggling dialogue, no references to being misunderstood or cries for acceptance, no cross-dressing, and only limited references to hard drinking. However, it's clearly possible to have a movie turn out this bizarre and laughably amateurish without any involvement from Edward D. Wood, Jr. That said, I encourage you to form your own opinion. Like all the titles within this book, we want you to enjoy this movie in your own way, alleged Ed Wood script or not.

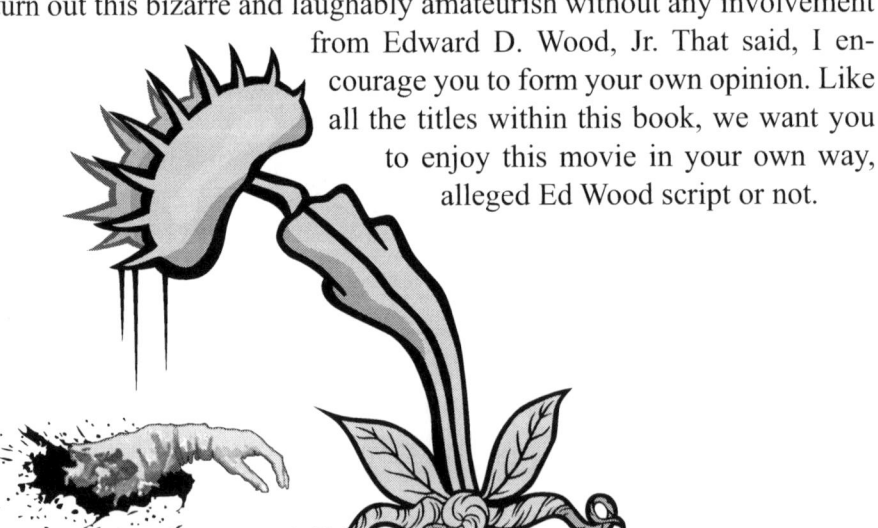

MANEATER OF HYDRA

1967

STEVEN B. ORKIN

Let's establish something right out of the gate. As cinephiles gather lists of the greatest films ever, *King Kong*, *Lawrence of Arabia*, *The Sound of Music*, and *The Wizard of Oz* will never have to glance nervously over their shoulders wondering if *Maneater of Hydra* is going to supplant (pun unintended) them on the list.

Directed by Mel Welles, it's a European production using various horror tropes, and is kind of a demented morality play mixed with Agatha Christie's novel, *And Then There Were None*. That said, there are a few affecting moments that make it watchable in an MST 3000 kind of way.

Our story begins on a European seafront, where the affable Alfredo (Ricardo Valle), gathers our cast and arranges transport to a nearby island. As he's driving them to the estate of the island's owner, the guest beside him, Cora Robinson (Kai Fischer), takes his hand, despite her husband, James (Rolf von Nauckhoff) being in back with the other guests. As you might imagine, Cora's sentence for being sexually assertive is death. Alfredo is likewise sentenced for being receptive to Cora's advances.

As they continue, Alfredo mentions that they "may be the first tourists on the island" and that the Baron "needs money for research." When

CINEMA BIZARRO

asked why the island seems deserted, Alfredo admits there was a "ridiculous vampire scare."

Moments after the abrasive Myrtle Callahan (Matilde Muñoz Sampedro) admonishes Alfredo to drive more carefully so she can take photos (a pastime she is pathological about), someone runs in front of their car. Intrepid guest David Moss (George Martin) confirms the man is dead and they notice a peculiar puncture mark on his face. David will, of course, live to see the film's credits for the virtue of being unflappably masculine.

The island's mysterious owner, Baron von Weser (Cameron Mitchell) appears, explaining that the man was his cook and had been driven mad by an illness. Assuring them the body will be retrieved, he leads them on foot to his villa.

Oh. By the way, Myrtle's sentence for being irritating will be death.

As they traverse the villa's gardens, quirky botanist Professor Julius Demerist (Hermann Nehlsen) stealthily grabs a soil sample and asks the Baron about the plants. For the sin of inquisitiveness, the good professor is thus doomed to… well, death, naturally.

The group gathers for dinner, and we learn that the Baron is a botanical geneticist, having altered cucumbers to taste like beef. The enterprising James suggests they could make a fortune selling the genetically modified vegetables (OMG, GMO's!), thus sentencing himself to death for the sin of capitalism.

The guests are later shocked by the dead cook reappearing, but the Baron explains it's his twin, Baldi (Mike Brendel), who will eventually die for the sin of unquestioning loyalty (at least until the Baron later betrays him).

Meanwhile, Alfredo, out in his car, becomes the film's first casualty. We never see what kills him, only that he is transfixed by it as it drains his life away.

As the rest of the group turns in, David chats outside with the last of the cast to speak, the winsome Beth Christiansen (Elisa Montés), advising her to lock her door and windows. Beth will survive the film's events for the virtue of being innocent and pretty.

The also-pretty, but not-very-innocent Cora, sensually dressed and

MANEATER OF HYDRA

barefoot, later sneaks out of her room and heads for Alfredo. It's implied she is followed by James, who was secretly awake when she left. Before she reaches Alfredo (and discovers he's dead), she notices the Baron in his lab and decides to seduce him instead. Finding the Baron impervious to her efforts, she glumly returns to the main house and is alone in her room when she later receives a visitation from whatever killed Alfredo. Unlike her would-be lover, Cora manages to belt out a scream before the scene fades to black. Why doesn't anyone else hear this? It's a mystery of the script. The next morning, James discovers her body, face scarred identically to Baldi's twin.

The Baron tells the anxious cast he'll contact authorities, but shockingly, the phone is dead. Further, the ferry that brought them isn't due for another day or two and the only boat on the island has been scuttled.

Dr. Demerist later meets with the Baron, informing him he "has proof" that one of his experiments has escaped his lab. Despite this, he offers to help report the results of his various experiments. The Baron refuses, menacingly telling the professor, "You're wrong about my experiments being out of control. I'm never out of control. Never." Maneuvering the shocked Demerist near a statue with a kill switch, the Baron placidly watches him die. Mourning period over, he summons the faithful Baldi to dispose of him, instructing him to "Use discretion. He was a nice man."

David spots Baldi carrying Demerist and accuses him of the murders. The Baron appears and promptly throws Baldi under the bus, asking him, "Why did you do it?" Baldi flees to the ruins of an old church where he climbs to the roof, hurling large, stone blocks at the two men before the neglected structure collapses, killing him.

Back at the house that night, Myrtle insists on taking photos of the coming storm. Assuming the danger has passed with Baldi's death, no one stops her. Soon after exiting the house, she notices the "maneater" extending its deadly limbs toward her. Though it's never stated, the plant presumably has a hypnotic effect on its prey, since no one ever runs from it once it gets close. It quickly dispatches Myrtle, leaving behind the odd, trademark facial scars.

Later, the cast discusses her whereabouts. Just after James goes upstairs to check her room, Beth spots her body outside. The maneater

CINEMA BIZARRO

promptly entraps her in its limbs. Inexplicably, she fares better than the other victims, struggling to free herself as she screams her head off, though her voice, like Myrtle's, is muted by the pre-storm winds.

James sees Beth being attacked from Myrtle's empty room and rushes downstairs, exclaiming "The tree is the killer, not Baldi!". Beth shrieks yet again, but this time, David hears her and grabs one of two large axes on the mantel. The Baron tries to stop him, but David overpowers him and rushes to Beth's aid, chopping at the tree's limbs, which drip blood as they're severed or injured. Once free, Beth, ever the delicate flower, promptly faints.

Meanwhile, the Baron, now unhinged and locked in combat with James, pushes him into the lethal spines of another of his experiments. To ensure that James is extra dead, he grabs the matching axe from the mantel, hacks him to pieces, then runs outside to defend his precious, maneater tree. However, he's not very good with moving targets, burying his axe in the maneater's trunk when David evades him. Overwhelmed with remorse at harming "his baby", he offers himself to his creation, which embraces and exsanguinates him, leaving him in a grotesque, scarred state, bound to the trunk of the dying tree as the credits roll.

Maneater of Hydra is decently paced and adequately acted, though the actors aren't given much to work with. They seem present solely to serve the script rather than embody actual people navigating incredible circumstances. Outside of Cameron Mitchell's ultimately deranged Baron, everyone behaves according to type.

As for the eponymous killer plant, it simply feeds on whatever it can get its limbs on. The effects representing it, its blossom-tipped limbs dripping with nectar, its stalks turning red as it drains its victims, are basic, but nevertheless have a weird, sickly erotic vibe that somehow lend the impression that done right, this film's premise could actually yield an authentically creepy and sinister result. Remake, anyone?

BRIDES OF BLOOD

1968

TRACY MERCER

Brides of Blood is a cinematic guilty pleasure of delight! Yes, a case could be made for it being a semi-sleazy, totally not politically-correct horror film — but it also delivers the cheesy goods with some silly humor and wonderful, if not schlocky, set pieces. And what's wrong with a little harmless, escapist fun? Gentle readers, if you accept the mission to watch this 1968 Filipino horror exploitation film for what it is, you are assured to have a blast. If you seek to watch this older gem through a post-2020 lens, well… you may be reaching for some pearls to clutch, and *Brides of Blood* may not be a suitable midnight movie adventure for you. Now that the stage has been properly set, let us begin our journey into the heart of Blood Island!

Let's start with the title. Or in this case, a series of titles. As best as experts can tell, the film we are celebrating was released as *The Brides of Blood Island*. It was released internationally as *Brides of Blood*. Depending on where you are reading this in the world, you can also find

CINEMA BIZARRO

this movie with alternate titles that include: *Brides of the Beast, Danger of Tiki Island,* and *Grave Desires*. Great titles all. Also of note, this film is the second in a four-Filipino-horror-film-spectacular produced by Eddie Romero and Kane W. Lynn that Monster Kids refer to as the "Blood Island" series. This gonzo four-part series includes the following titles: *Terror is a Man, The Mad Doctor of Blood Island,* and *Beast of Blood*. Pfew! Glad we are now all operating from the same foundational baseline.

Our gloriously garish tale of adventure begins with three Americans arriving ashore on a tropical island paradise. We meet Dr. Paul Henderson, played by former 1930's/40's B-movie king, Kent Taylor. We learn Paul is a scientist investigating atomic bomb test radiation effects on the island's flora and fauna. He appears to be so concerned with science that he's totally sexually uninterested in his va-va-voom, much-too-young for him wife, Carla, played by Beverly Powers, who is credited in this film as "Beverly Hills". Sexually frustrated Carla is introduced to the audience cheating on her husband with one of the members of the boat taking them to Paul's island of interest. It's almost like this woman has never seen a horror film that tells us promiscuous ladies may not live through the movie's run time. Somehow, a scene that is awkward as can be works because Beverly is a wonderful B-movie presence that owns the screen. Fun factoid: Beverly was a famous burlesque artist who started her career in the Tropicana chorus at the Sands Hotel in Las Vegas at 17 (!) before transitioning to a striptease artist billed as Miss Beverly Hills, playing to great fanfare at the Largo Club on the Sunset Strip back in the day. Our third American character is a Peace Corps rep named Jim Farrell, played by B-picture matinee idol, John Ashley, whose handsome visage might best be known for gracing American International Pictures like *Dragstrip Girl* and *Motorcycle Gang* before transitioning to being a producer/actor of TV series, including *The A-Team*.

After the captain of the boat informs our three Americans (and audience) that the island is cursed and referred to as "Blood Island", we learn that the trio will be trapped on the island, as no boats show up for months at a time. Our Americans' first glimpse of the local natives takes the form of a funeral where two totally dismembered female bodies are seen being taken out to sea. What exactly is going on here?

Cut to: An island local invites the Americans to trek to the palatial estate of rich guy, Esteban Powers. While gorgeous and youthful, Powers tells his guests that he's actually fifty years old. He alludes that the tribal population on the island is fine, post-atomic tests, but the local island fauna seems to be experiencing mutation and odd changes. Unsettled, our trio heads back to the village where they are staying, but along the way, chaos breaks out when Carla is attacked by a very phallic banana tree while a butterfly seems to turn into a vampire and bites Paul on the hand. Both escape with their lives, confounded by the surreal events. It seems strange things are indeed afoot on Blood Island.

The film next leans further into exploitation movie tropes when we see two local village women who are offered as tribal sacrifices, tied to an altar, stripped naked, and assaulted by a hideous humanoid beast who tears them limb from limb. Several years later, Roger Corman's *Humanoids from the Deep* (1980) has several sequences that are shot in similar fashion and framing. It seems the local villagers sacrifice a few of their women periodically to satisfy the creature sexually so he will not destroy the entire village out of frustration. "It needs only women, he satisfies himself on them," we are told.

Paul slowly comes to understand that the animals in paradise have the ability to transform into monstrous versions of themselves. Meanwhile, there is lust-at-first-sight between a local tribal girl named Alma and Peace Corps Jim. Wouldn't you know it, Alma is entered into a "lottery" scheme to potentially be the next of two women who could be sacrificed to the monster that keeps the locals living in fear. Concurrently, Paul and his friends attempt to learn more from the wealthy Esteban about this mysterious island. That proves especially hard as Esteban suffers from debilitating migraines and seems to foreshadow that he's more than a little unhinged.

Esteban retreats to his bedroom and we see him tossing and turning violently in bed. We get a better sense of Esteban's fortress and note he has a lot of "little people" servants who are treated with zero respect and who would also get him cancelled in contemporary Hollywood.

The important story-beats to know: Jim figures out that his would-be love interest Alma (who is about as interesting and non-dimensional as Charlton Heston's mute, would-be girlfriend, Nova in the original

CINEMA BIZARRO

Planet of the Apes) is to be sacrificed next to the island's monster for "the greater good". But it turns out, chivalry is not dead as Jim rises up and saves his island girl-crush. Backstory beats come into focus when Esteban reveals he and his wife were exposed to radiation during the atomic bomb testing. She died, he lived, and now he is the mutated, sexual predator, island monster! Carla, only because the script tells her to, follows Esteban into the jungle to be violently dismembered by a tree in a sequence that must be seen to be believed. Esteban a.k.a. the monster, is dispatched by the villagers with fire like films have been doing since 1931's *Frankenstein*. And, in one of the craziest endings this side of *Dirty Dancing*, this exploitation horror film ends on an extended and intricate dance sequence followed by our lovers Jim and Alma making an exit into the jungle. What a bloody good time! If we are ever lucky enough to get an American remake of *Brides of Blood*, Channing Tatum should be cast as Jim so he can star as a perfect mix of his *Magic Mike* meets *The Lost City* self, attempting to top the final gonzo scene of this 1968 cult classic.

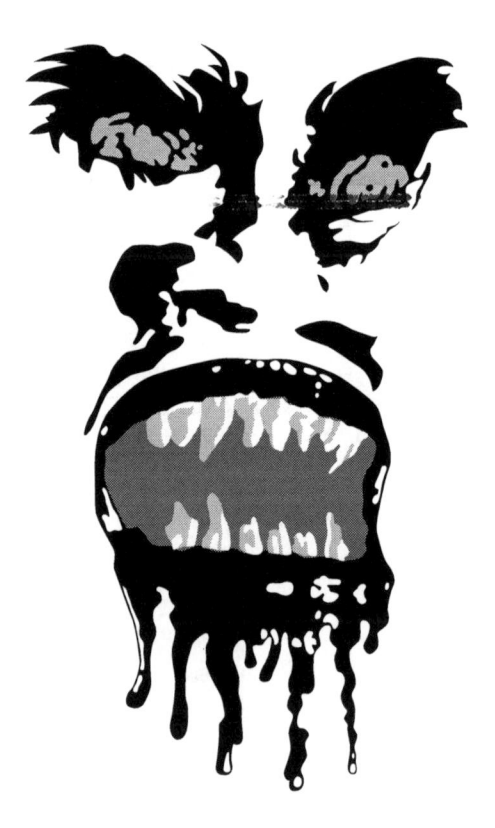

ROBOT MONSTER

1953

PHOEF SUTTON

You know this movie even if you've never seen it. It's the one with the man wearing a gorilla suit with a diving helmet on his head. It's the poster child for Bad Movies.

During the Bad Movie Boom of the late '70s and early '80s, brothers Harry and Michael Medved anointed Phil Tucker's magnum opus with the Golden Turkey for "Most Ridiculous Movie Monster" in their 1980 book, *The Golden Turkey Awards*. Two years earlier, Harry Medved and Randy Dreyfuss published, *The Fifty Worst Films of All Time*, naming *Robot Monster* one of those fifty. As a young man, I bought those books. Like everyone else, I laughed at the incompetence of those would-be filmmakers, like Phil Tucker and Ed Wood and William "One Shot" Beaudine, who had the temerity to think that they could actually make movies.

It was only later that I realized these films had a lot going for them. This "laughing at" as a "gateway drug" to appreciation isn't new. I recall, as a child, watching *Fractured Flickers*. Produced in the early 60s by the great Jay Ward (*Bullwinkle*), *Fractured Flickers* was a half-hour show that pieced together clips from silent films and over-dubbed them with humorous dialogue. Hans Conried would host, say, a truncated showing of Lon Chaney's *The Hunchback of Notre Dame*, but it would be presented as "Dinkey Dunstan, Boy Cheerleader" and transformed into a comedy. At the time, I thought this was the funniest thing ever. When, years later, I saw the uncut Chaney film, I felt guilty about laughing at it years before. But maybe that was just my "way into" silent films. Laugh at them first, then grow to appreciate them.

It's much the same with "bad" movies. Maybe you need the Medveds to enjoy them first. Then, as you watch them, you grow to appreciate them for what they really are. My experience with *Robot Monster* typified this journey. The first time I saw it was on Washington DC local TV. It more than lived up to its reputation. There was the gorilla suit. There was the diving helmet. There was the bubble machine. There was all the glorious, overwritten dialogue. It was sublimely ridiculous, and I loved it.

Cut to much later. I was living in Los Angeles. I was married and had a daughter who was a second-generation Monster Kid. I noticed they were holding a 3-D film festival at the Egyptian Theater in Hollywood. I decided to take Celia to see *Robot Monster* on the big screen, in 3 Dimensions. The way it was meant to be seen.

It was a revelation.

The movie opens with 10-year-old Johnny (Gregory Moffett) playing with his younger sister (Pamela Paulson) in the environs of Griffith Park's Bronson Caves. He is playing Spaceman and wearing a toy astronaut's helmet. His sister wants to play house, but he only wants to disintegrate her with his ray gun.

He meets two archeologists (as you do) who are digging in the cave. One, the Professor (John Mylong), is an older man with a foreign accent. The other is Roy (George Nader), a young hunk. When Johnny points his ray gun at them and tells them they must die, the Professor says it would be better for them to live in peace. Then Johnny's big sister, Alice (Claudia Barrett) shows up and makes the children go take a nap, which Johnny resents.

It is when Johnny takes his nap that the story really starts. The bulk of the film is Johnny's pre-adolescent dream of destruction and lust. And it's awesome.

It starts with Johnny "waking up," going back to the now-empty cave and getting struck by lightning followed by quick cuts of dinosaurs fighting (lifted from 1940's *One Million B.C.*). When Johnny recovers from his lightning strike, the world has been destroyed. What's more, there's scientific equipment in the cave. And a bubble making machine. Oh, and a man in a gorilla suit with a space helmet on his head. This is Ro-Man Extension XJ-2 (George Barrows), vanguard of an alien invasion.

Now, a word about this setting, because this is the main reason this film is ridiculed. The equipment looks like a pile of junk from your father's garage, all stacked on top of an end table from your bedroom. The bubble machine makes no sense at all, but in the 3D presentation the bubbles did jump out of the screen in an impressive manner. What creates the most lasting memory is Ro-Man himself. The shaggy gorilla suit and the "diving helmet" have gone down in bad movie history.

But remember, this is the dream of a ten-year-old boy who was just wearing a space helmet and using a toy ray gun. What's more natural than that he should use what's around him to try to make sense of his life? Why wouldn't he create a mix of gorilla and spaceman? Why wouldn't he fill his invader's cave with junk from his father's garage?

As the dream progresses, the screenplay by Wyott Ordung, gets more and more bizarre. Johnny overhears Ro-Man conversing with his leader, The Great Guidance, (both impressively voiced by John Brown) saying that they have already wiped out the human race. There are only a few people left alive on Earth. Ro-Man is tasked by his leader with eliminating the rest of them.

Johnny runs back to his family with the news that they are being sought out by the Ro-Man. The family is holed up in the ruins of their city (This was impressively filmed in the wreckage of Chavez Ravine, a largely Hispanic community that was torn down in order to build Dodger Stadium). The Professor is now the de facto father of the family and has built an electric barricade to protect them from being seen by Ro-Man. Ro-Man contacts them and offers them a painless death if they surrender. If they don't, their death will be "indescribable."

Though the invaders seem invincible, the Ro-Man begins to doubt himself when he can't find the remaining pesky humans. The Great Guidance says he's not acting like a "Ro-Man" but rather like a "human." The Ro-man's increasing confusion seems to reflect young Johnny's confusion about the world, his place in the world, and his burgeoning sexual awareness. Now, before you roll your eyes at that, consider what follows.

The Ro-Man develops an interest in Alice and asks her to meet him ("Is Ro-Man going on a date with Alice?" the little sister asks). Alice agrees to go, offering her honor to preserve the human race. Johnny runs off in her stead and confronts Ro-Man, telling him he "looks like a pooped out pinwheel," an immortal line that will live forever in movie history. Meanwhile, Roy and Alice "play house" and get married. The Ro-Man strangles Johnny's little sister (off-screen) but becomes increasingly confused by his feelings for Alice. He abducts her, under orders to kill her "with his hands" (and kudos to George Barrows, the actor in the gorilla suit who has to trudge across an endless, arid landscape holding actress Clauia Barret in his furry arms). His feelings for Alice get the better of him. He must kill her, but he can't. "At what point on the graph do 'must' and 'cannot' meet?" he asks himself. That line alone perfectly captures the angst of a pre-adolescent boy faced with manhood.

So, sitting in the Egyptian Theater, I realized that *Robot Monster*, far from being the worst film ever made, is actually a rather deep movie. In fact, with an impressive early score by the great Elmer Bernstein, I'd venture to say it's one of the best films of the 1950s.

So, take that, brothers Medved!

THE QUATERMASS XPERIMENT

1955

STEVEN PEROS

Professor Bernard Quatermass. He has been an admitted inspiration to, and influence on, Stephen King, John Carpenter, Guillermo Del Toro, individual members of The Beatles, Pink Floyd, and Monty Python, and that's just the tip of the Quatermass. If you enjoy serialized one-hour dramas with their cliffhanger endings, you have Professor Quatermass to thank. If you have found a place in your horror-filled heart for all things Hammer Films, which launched Christopher Lee and Peter Cushing to international stardom, you have the feisty Professor to thank.

Quatermass is a character created by 31-year-old British writer Nigel Kneale, under contract to the BBC, in a six-part, serialized, science fiction program called *The Quatermass Experiment*, broadcast live in the UK over six weeks in the summer of 1953. Brilliant, opinionated yet open-minded, smarter than anyone in the room (but first to admit when he is not), Quatermass is the head of the fictitious British Experimental Rocket Group. It was the BBC's first foray into sci-fi, brought in 3.4 million viewers to the first episode, and roughly 5 million to the final episode, disproving network opinion that science fiction would only deliver a "niche" television audience and was more suitable for the big screen and big budgets. The tightly-budgeted program's cliffhanger format was also new to television dramas and became the model in the UK thereafter, ultimately influencing television in America and globally, notably the BBC's own *Doctor Who*.

Enter Hammer Films of London, which began negotiating for the film rights after the third episode aired. Founded in 1934 and existing largely on an output of dramas and crime-thrillers shown primarily in the UK, many film historians will hastily claim that 1957's *Curse of Frankenstein* was the breakout international success that finally announced Hammer as a new major player in horror cinema. The fact is their true breakout horror film, albeit sci-fi/horror, was their feature film adaptation of Kneale's BBC serial, retitled *The Quatermass Xperiment* by Hammer to boldly embrace the recently created "X" Certificate (For viewers 16 and over ONLY!) they were hopeful the BBFC (British Board of Film Classification) would slap on the finished product. And they were right.

As two young people make out in a car in a rural area of England, a spaceship crash-lands nearby. Enter the police, ambulances, and Quatermass, whose Rocket Group had sent the doomed ship into space. This was Hammer's first big change: the very British Quatermass was now played by American actor, Brian Donlevy, as per Hammer's financing partner, who insisted on an American name in order to sell the movie in the US. This was not unusual for Hammer, who would often insert an inexpensive US Hollywood actor in the lead role, as they did with the likes of Lloyd Bridges, Robert Preston, and Dan Duryea in earlier films, to aid in marquee value. This practice would be phased out after UK actors like Christopher Lee and Peter Cushing ascended to international fame in their own right, and Hammer's "Britishness" became part of its global allure.

When the authorities open the door of the downed spaceship, only one astronaut tumbles out, Victor Caroon (Richard Wordsworth). The other two are nowhere to be found; only their empty space uniforms. Caroon is in a state of shock and kept under private observation by Quatermass and his colleague, Dr. Briscoe (David King-Wood). Only Caroon's wife, Judith (American actress, Margia Dean, then girlfriend of co-financier Robert Lippert) is allowed to be at his side.

While Quatermass joins forces with church-going Police Inspector Lomax (Jack Warner) to find out what happened to the other two astronauts, Judith orchestrates Caroon's escape with the aid of a friend who poses as a male nurse. Prior to the escape, Caroon deliberately uses his fist to smash a potted cactus in his room, causing it to fuse with his arm. This deadly appendage is used to kill the phony male nurse, allowing Caroon to escape into the night. The nurse is found with his face gruesomely mutilated and body seemingly "deflated", undoubtedly earning the film its "X" certificate.

In the meantime, Quatermass, Lomax, and Briscoe deduce that Caroon's ship had intercepted some form of energy from space that dissolved/absorbed the other two astronauts and is now using Caroon as its host, transforming him, bit by bit, into a new alien life-form. In a zoo sequence often compared in eeriness to the US work of creative producer Val Lewton, particularly 1942's *Cat People*, Caroon stalks the caged animals and ultimately feeds on a lion. As praised by *Halloween* director John Carpenter, "The zoo sequence is just about as good as it gets." In the aftermath, Quatermass & Co find traces at the zoo of a spore-like life-form which reproduces at an alarming rate and could devour all life on earth if left unchecked.

In an earlier scene, Caroon is approached by a little girl (future successful actress and Paul McCartney girlfriend, Jane Asher) who he resists killing for sustenance, smashing her doll but sparing her life.

Best to detour at this point to sing the praises of actor Richard Wordsworth, cast as Caroon by director Val Guest because of his stage experience and here making his film debut. With subtle but effective makeup by Hammer's resident monster maker, Phil Leakey, it is a remarkably expressive performance, with no dialogue, often bringing accurate comparisons to Boris Karloff's work in 1931's *Frankenstein*. Yes, it's THAT good.

Ultimately, Wordsworth-as-Caroon is no more as he is fully transformed into a tentacled alien creature (actual tripe was used in its creation by Hammer's special effects genius, Les Bowie) perched atop a scaffolding in Westminster Abbey. Quatermass hits on the idea to electrocute it, which could decimate the abbey, but in typical Quatermass fashion, he is willing to take that risk. After the creature has been effectively fried, Quatermass is asked what comes next, to which he replies in no uncertain terms, "We're going to start again," as he then walks off alone down the street in and out of lamp lights. A rocket ship launching is our final image.

CINEMA BIZARRO

Under contract to the BBC, Kneale was unavailable to adapt his 200-minute TV drama into an 82-minute feature. Hammer hired American screenwriter Richard Landau, who was rewritten by Guest, known primarily for comedies. Kneale, who by all accounts was a dissatisfied curmudgeon from a young age, disliked the casting of Donlevy and much of the adaptation, though he did like Guest's direction overall.

Kneale felt casting an American was all wrong and Donlevy too much of a bulldog, from first scene to last. The British director, Guest, liked Donlevy and thought him better than having a typical British professorial-type in the part. Ultimately Andrew Kier would later make the perfect Quatermass (British, tough, intelligent, good-humored) in the third, final, and best film in Hammer's Quatermass series, 1967's *Quatermass and the Pit*, covered by this writer in the first book in this series, *Giant Bug Cinema*.

Guest later explained that he wanted to make the film "science fact" not "science fiction". Thus, it is often shot handheld, like a newsreel, particularly the exterior location work. Guest works wonders within tight budget constraints. For example, in the opening, the sound of the spacecraft, the edits, the wind, all replace actually seeing the craft in the sky or witnessing a costly actual crash.

The Quatermass Xperiment is an intense, memorable film, somehow filled with a mood of absolute dread while simultaneously being a solid entertainment. Hammer's Anthony Hinds bet on the right horse, including his atypical choice of director. This same team would move on to a next Quatermass film, this time with the participation of Nigel Kneale, but for more on *Quatermass 2*, read on…

THE CRAWLING EYE

1958

MIKE PEROS

The first time I watched *The Trollenberg Terror* (retitled for the US as *The Crawling Eye*), it was for one big reason. It had nothing to do with Jimmy Sangster, the film's author and future director of horror films like 1970's *The Horror of Frankenstein* and *Lust for a Vampire*, or the prospect of seeing a monster that resembled... a crawling eye (really, it looks like a land-locked octopus with a huge eye and a few pesky tentacles). Instead, it had to do with the film's lead, Forrest Tucker. As a young fella growing up in the 1960's, I was a fan of *F Troop*, a TV comedy that ran for a few seasons and depicted the cavalry and Indians in a wacky love-hate relationship. Presiding over the hijinks was Forrest Tucker's gruff and resourceful Sgt. O' Rourke. I enjoyed Tucker's work, particularly his self-assurance and comic timing. After the show was canceled, Tucker was good and menacing opposite John Wayne's *Chisum* (1970). Then, in 1973, my brothers and I got to meet Tucker when he and a few show-biz veterans (including Donald O'Connor, Gloria DeHaven, and "Crazy Guggenheim" aka Frank Fontane) toured the provinces, including Commack, Long Island, in would-be impresario (soon to be murdered) Roy Radin's Vaudeville Shows. Tucker performed a mildly amusing monologue, did a song or two, then ambled offstage — later, we were able to get his autograph, wherein we noticed that he didn't seem particularly happy to be on this tour.

CINEMA BIZARRO

Still, I remained a fan, and caught *The Crawling Eye* when I was a mere lad, after being alerted to its airing by that essential publication, *TV Guide*. The 1958 release was a good ten years before *F Troop*, and the same year that Tucker impressed with his comic chops as the boisterous, filthy rich Beauregard opposite Rosalind Russell's *Auntie Mame*. In *The Crawling Eye*, Tucker is restrained but effective, playing United Nations troubleshooter Alan Brooks, on his way to Switzerland's (fictional) Mount Trollenberg because of some mysterious climbing accidents.

The British-made thriller has a nifty pre-credits sequence with some mountain climbers discovering that one of their group has been killed, with his head ripped off. The credits on most available prints display its original title *The Trollenberg Terror*, but it was not only retitled for its American release but cut from 84 minutes to 75 minutes (Americans need to see those monsters sooner!). The film introduces the three main characters, all on the same Swiss train: "psychic" sisters Sarah (Jennifer Payne) and Anne (Janet Munro), and Alan Brooks (Forrest Tucker). Anne takes one look at the Trollenberg sign and passes out in the arms of the nearby Brooks, who is bound for Trollenberg, but the revived younger sister Anne insists they get off there, too.

It's not long before Trollenberg's dour Mayor Klein (Frederick Schiller) tells the travelers that tourism is way down — amazing what a few mysterious deaths will do. While Klein insists "All these stories are nonsense," even he's not convinced. Inquisitive journalist, Philip Truscott (Lawrence Payne) brushes up on Brooks and the psychic sisters, whose mindreading act became "real" once Anne developed "powers." Anne can't help staring at that mountain, as she feels "It's all there." And as questions abound about that pre-credit discovery of the headless body, two geologists, Dewhurst (Stuart Saunders) and Brett (Andrew Faulds), plan to climb Trollenberg to search for answers.

When Brooks visits his old friend, Professor Crevett (Warren Mitchell) at the observatory, he tells Brooks of several accidents wherein the bodies have disappeared — and then, there's that persistent radioactive cloud at the south face of Trottenberg. Crevett wants Brooks to use his standing with the United Nations to allow him to call in a special team. However, Brooks is reluctant, as he had been discredited in an earlier

THE CRAWLING EYE

effort: "I'm not going to stick my neck out, like I did in the Andes."

While the intrepid Dewhurst and Brett have reached the climbers' hut atop Trollenberg, they are unaware that the cloud is moving in their direction. Anne says that one of them is "the one". Not "the fat one" (Dewhurst) but "the other one" (Brett). When this cuts to a lean, transfixed Brett leaving the hut, it's clear that Anne can 'see' what's transpiring on the mountain. Brooks phones Dewhurst, and Dewhurst confirms there is no sign of Brett, but after hearing a noise, Dewhurst foolishly opens the hut door (I know it's 1957, but haven't they learned by now??), sees something frightening and screams his head off (Well, not literally... not yet.).

After a rescue team (including Brooks) finds Dewhurst's decapitated body in the hut, one of the rescuers later spots a rucksack further up with the missing head. Alas for rescuer #1 (and the follow-up rescuer), Brett savagely kills them both in one of the film's most effective scenes. A hot and sweaty Brett later shows up in the village, appearing lost and uncoordinated (he cannot hold his glass of liquor). When Brett sees Anne, he attacks her, but Brooks knocks him out, yet there is no blood from Brett's head wound (perhaps he is "the walking dead"). Undeterred, Brett tries again and this time Brooks shoots him dead, with the ultra-dead Brett's flesh freezing, then decomposing.

Finally, Brooks, Crevett, and Truscott put some of it together: the similarity to the Andes incident, as it too, included a psychic who was viewed as a threat (and in the Andes incident, later killed), the possibility that this persistent radioactive "mist" is from another galaxy, and needs thinner atmospheres to survive.

Since the cloud is making its move, all decide to head to the fortified observatory for protection. But wouldn't you know, a mother is looking for her missing child (mothers should really be more attentive to their children), who is naturally in harm's way. Brooks stays behind to find her, and we get our first glimpse of the monster that appears to be the misbegotten alien sibling to the sea creature from *Reap the Wild Wind* (1942). While the "crawling eye" does have tentacles, they aren't good for "closing the deal," as Brooks is able to rescue the child rather easily. Though the monster gives the fleeing villagers a scare (when its mist freezes the motors), all are able to make it back.

By now, the mist has split up into five "crawling eyes", laying siege to the observatory. In addition, one of the earlier rescuers, a now-sweaty Hans (Colin Douglas), tries to kill Anne. With three attempts on her life in twenty-four hours, Anne is not having her best day. This results in an intense struggle between Hans and Brooks, and the victorious Brooks realizes that these wailing creatures have their own Achilles' heel: intense heat. Luckily, between the planes Brooks has ordered and some convenient firebombs, wielded expertly by Brooks and Truscott, they're able to destroy these monsters and that ever-present mist, once and for all. There's even a hint of a romance between Truscott and Anne — and for Sarah and Brooks.

The Trollenberg Terror/The Crawling Eye has much going for it. The performances are uniformly good, especially from Tucker, Janet Munro, Lawrence Payne, and Andrew Faulds. The film also generally manages to transcend its "B" status with effective direction from Quentin Lawrence, a screenplay from Jimmy Sangster that skillfully blends shock and suspense, and fine camerawork from Monty Berman, all working in tandem to sustain an air of mystery and foreboding. But when the mist materializes into the "crawling eye," we not only see the limitations of the budget but also of the "monster." It's good at knocking down buildings but when it comes to getting hold of humans, it's downright inept. In its final section, the monster, as well as the movie, loses its grip. Like many horror films before and since, the monster was more frightening when we couldn't see it.

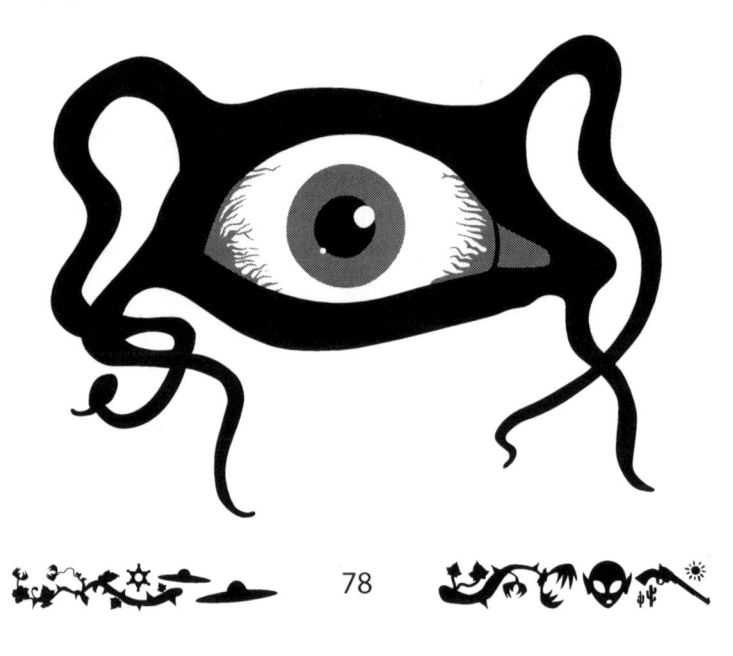

WARNING FROM SPACE

1956/1963

BRIAN R. SOLOMON

In the wake of the success of *Godzilla,* the giant monster who stomped Tokyo and paradoxically won the hearts of millions, Japan entered into what was called the "*tokusatsu* boom" — a period from the late 1950's through the 1960's when moviegoers seemingly couldn't get enough of science fiction special effects movies. It was a golden age for fantastical cinema, when Japan would actually be on the cutting edge of that genre. But they were also finding their way in the beginning, and it took a while to really coalesce, during an early period when the studios were still trying to figure it out. *Warning from Space* was a product of that period.

Gojira, the original 1954 film that introduced the giant lizard to the world, had been produced by Toho Co., which instantly became an industry leader in the *tokusatsu* genre. And one of their leading competitors, Daiei Film, would eventually figure out a way to compete with them with a giant monster of their own, the infamous, titanic, flying turtle known as Gamera. The studio also became known for the *Zatoichi* samurai pictures, as well as the folkloric *Daimajin* trilogy. But before any of that, they took their first stab at science fiction with a film originally known as *Uchūjin Tōkyō nirawaru*, roughly translated as the typically literal *Spacemen Appear in Tokyo*.

To Daiei's credit, it would be the first Japanese *tokusatsu* movie produced in color, beating out Toho's excellent *The Mysterians* by a year. A strange and unusual blend of several genres, it represents a formative phase in the development of effects flicks in Japan, and can be a jarring watch, although it has many things to recommend it. Unlike so many similar films to come, it would keep the emphasis strongly on the human characters, placing them in an interesting and believable world that looks and feels like Japanese city life in the 1950's. At times, the titular "spacemen" — known as Pairans in the movie — seem to take a backseat, which can be a positive or a negative, depending on your own preferences.

Masaichi Nagata, the head of Daiei, had made a name for his studio producing high-end films like Akira Kurosawa's *Rashomon* (1957), and Teinosuke Kinugasa's *Gate of Hell*, which won a 1953 Academy Award for Best Foreign Language Film. But after the success of *Gojira*, he wanted to try something different, and optioned a novel about alien invasion by Gentaro Nakajima, then hired the accomplished screenwriter Hideo Oguni, who had worked on the scripts for prestigious Kurosawa films like *Ikiru* (1952) and *The Seven Samurai* (1954), to help translate it to the screen. Veteran helmsman Koji Shima, who had been a renowned leading man on screen in Japanese cinema of the 1920's and '30's prior to taking to the director's chair in 1939, was next brought on board.

The result is a sometimes engaging and always quirky film that deals for the first time with what would eventually become a typical Japanese sci-fi trope: alien interlopers on planet Earth. Thankfully, in this case, they are friendly — here to warn us and protect us from Planet R, a rogue heavenly body on a collision course with our own. Today, the film is probably best remembered for these aliens and their unique design — the work of avant-garde artist Taro Okamoto — featuring a star-shaped costume with a single giant eye in the center (a design that would be outright cribbed four years later by DC Comics when they introduced

WARNING FROM SPACE

Justice League nemesis Starro and the Star Conquerors in the pages of *The Brave and the Bold* #28.)

Somewhat disappointingly, the Pairans in their true form are only seen briefly in the movie, but they make the most of it, as the surreal scenes aboard their spaceship feature one of the earliest examples of a fictional alien language in film, subtitled in Japanese. It's also worth noting that although the Pairans are human-sized in the film — essentially actors in star-shaped leotards — the posters produced to advertise the movie depicted them as towering creatures terrorizing the city — no doubt another attempt to capitalize on *Gojira/Godzilla*.

The Pairans are also seen (inadvertently) terrorizing Japanese citizens as they try to make initial contact in several horror-tinged scenes that are reminiscent of George Pal's *War of the Worlds* (1953). For the most part, they appear in mutated human form, specifically in the form of pop star Hikari Aozora, played by the striking Toyomi Karita. The majority of the film is carried by dour, yet likeable figures like astronomer Dr. Kamura (Bontaro Miake) and news reporter Hoshino (Toshiyuki Obara), who run around dutifully and seriously, trying to save the world like so many of their scientist and journalist counterparts in American genre films of the same period.

The plot is almost childlike in its conception — the kind of movie where everyone important to the story seems to coincidentally know each other and live within reasonable distance of each other, and in which everyone does exactly what needs to be done at all times, although the requisite romantic subplot between Dr. Kamura's daughter Taeko (Mieko Nagai) and a similarly serious yet younger scientist, Dr. Toru Itsobe (Keizo Kawasaki) occasionally lightens up the proceedings. There is also a gangster subplot thrown in towards the end for good measure, making this movie an interesting genre mashup for its time.

In many ways, *Warning from Space* would set the tone for many of the Japanese science fiction films that followed, with its admonitions of doom for the human race and its urging for international cooperation, although unlike most films that typically condemned nuclear weaponry, in this film, the world's nuclear arsenal is actually put to good use in the attempt to divert or destroy Planet R before it impacts with Earth.

With its threat of an impending celestial collision, the film clearly was an influence on Toho's superior *Gorath* (1962), which in turn influenced much later films like Michael Bay's *Armageddon* (1998). Some similarities can even be seen in the Godzilla movie, *Invasion of Astro-Monster* (1965). The ingenious spaceship model work, as well as the film's unorthodox alien intelligences, also reportedly had a strong impact on Stanley Kubrick, who would later cite *Warning from Space* as one of the inspirations for *2001: A Space Odyssey* (1968).

Perhaps owing to its strangeness, or the fact that such pictures had not really been produced by Japan before, the movie was unable to find interest among American distributors at the time. In fact, it went unreleased in the United States until 1963, when it got its English title and received a very minor and short theatrical run. The film wouldn't really find an audience in the English-speaking world until 1967, when American International Pictures brought it to television and it started on its way to becoming a syndicated and late-night TV cult classic.

Japanese *tokusatsu* cinema would only get better in the ensuing decade and a half, and while *Warning from Space* is not the finest example of the genre at its peak, it is an entertaining and amusing artifact that helped to establish many of its tropes and techniques. And if nothing else, it helped to establish Daiei as a major player in the business of science-fiction filmmaking, thus setting the stage for even more memorable fare in the years to come.

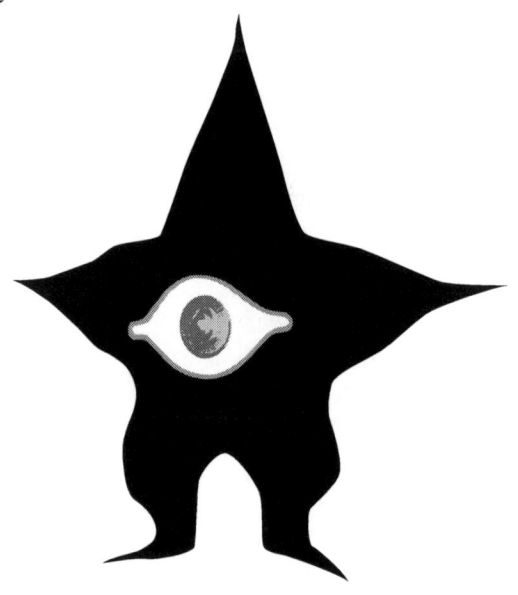

KRONOS
1957

NADIA ROBERTSON

A black & white spectacle born amid the golden days of science fiction, *Kronos* feels like a film tailor-made for a fun night out at the drive-in theater. Liberated from all seriousness by a breezy plot, *Kronos* is a perfect date night movie where copious amounts of stock footage, technical mumbo jumbo, and an onslaught of b-roll military strikes won't lose audiences in complexities as they sneak off mid-screening to grab concessions or get sidetracked sucking face with a sweetie.

The sci-fi scene of the 1950's saw silver screens saturated with stress-inducing images of hovering spacecrafts and extraterrestrials attempting to enslave or stamp out the human race for the survival of their own species. America's fascination with celestial curiosities, combined with a fixation on Communist "double agent" angst, had Americans simultaneously looking at the sky and over their shoulders. This climate resulted in a concentration of cinematic themes of widespread conspiracies that "invaders walk among us and want our stuff", leading to an obsession begetting an opportunistic boom in the mass production of the genre. What better way to comfortably confront your fears than to project them onto the biggest screen possible, sugarcoated under the guise of fluff entertainment?

Tapping into hot topics to produce a slew of movies with major profit potential, studios took advantage of siphoning off pop culture relevancy regarding top secret UFO projects and Cold War paranoia that sent

CINEMA BIZARRO

Americans down a spiral of conspiracies, flocking to films for validation of their shared anxieties. *Kronos* satisfies audience expectations while offering up some subtext, giving the people a lagniappe of cultural depth presented by way of playful B-movie panache. *Kronos* director, Kurt Neumann (who a year later would helm *The Fly*) performs movie magic despite dwindling funds forcing script rewrites, delivering pure pulp fiction on a tight, two-week schedule set by distribution company, Regal Films under 20th Century-Fox. Shot on a widescreen "Regalscope" format, the sense of space accentuates Kronos' monolithic stature so that the larger-than-life metallic monster appears to tower over landscapes now cast in the shadow of the looming foreign structure.

Cinematographer Karl Struss (1927's *Sunrise*, 1931's *Dr. Jekyll and Mr. Hyde*, 1932's *Island of Lost Souls*, 1940's *The Great Dictator*, and many more) supplies a seasoned skillset to guide the low budget visuals towards grandeur. Sound engineer James Mobley creates a chillingly alien soundscape, while stop-motion animator Wah Chang (of *Star Trek* designer fame) brings the mechanical movement of Kronos to believably convincing life. SFX specialists Irving Block, Jack Rabin, and Louis DeWitt worked as a trinity of creative collaborators connected through their own independent optics company. Rabin and DeWitt had previously joined up on *The Night of the Hunter* (1955) and *The Killing* (1956), while Block wrote the story for both *Kronos* and MGM's *Forbidden Planet* (1956). Teaming together their trifecta of effects expertise, they cook up a striking array of shoestring VFX.

The titular titan, fallen from the stars, resembles an iconic "flying saucer" as its aircraft zooms across the horizon, but unbeknownst to humans is that the spaceship actually harbors the body of a walking building (dubbed an "accumulator") aimed at absorbing all of Earth's available energy. After zapping a nearby motorist, Kronos herds its possessed human host towards the nearest government facility to transfer its sly sentience to the head of operations, Dr. Hubbel Eliot (John Emery), whose name surely nods to Harvey Hubbell, inventor of many electrical patents, and Edwin Hubble, whose cosmic discoveries eventually led to dedicating the Hubble Space telescope in his honor. Also stationed at the desert depot is a super computer specified as S.U.S.I.E (short for "Syncho-Unifying Sinometric Integrating Equitensor" - whatever that is), monitored by Dr. Leslie Gaskell, played by Jeff Morrow (a genre-juggling actor who thrived in science fiction, most notably, *This Island Earth*) and Dr. Arnold Culver (George O'Hanlon, voice of famous father from the future, George Jetson), who incorrectly analyzes the aerial activity to be a new asteroid instead of confirming alien life - whoops, what an oversight!

With the help of Vera Hunter (Barbara Lawrence), Dr. Gaskell's lab assistant "with benefits", the trio survey the astronomical anomaly to track its trajectory, as the object appears to display awareness beyond that of just a meteor. Operating under the control of Kronos, Dr. Eliot refers to an official list of nuclear power plants to guide the monstrous mammoth to the nearest substation so it can soak up energy for the sake of restoring the depleted power on its home planet. Manipulating officials to respond rashly with bomb blasts that unfortunately serve to only supersize Kronos's strength, fools are made of the scientists responsible for engineering the same nuclear energy keeping Kronos going, and going, and going... theoretically until it transmits out every last electron available on Earth. Damned to return to a Digital Dark Age, mankind must suffer the symptoms of a society absent of smartphones as we go mad from Wi-Fi withdrawal, lest the "Ravager of Worlds" be stopped. Kronos may lack an "off" switch, but pseudoscience saves the day when the stumped scientists surmise that if their own supercomputer can run the risk of overloading, then *of course* "the polarity can be reversed", resulting in Kronos essentially eating itself alive - ironically imploding the alien by the very power that propels it.

Giant monster movies thrived throughout the 1950's, their big box office numbers proving the genre a lucrative investment for studios eager to earn easy money from crowd-pleasing pictures while still alluding to deeper allegories on current affairs. The American edit of *Godzilla: King of the Monsters* (1956) had hit the US a year before *Kronos*, depicting a manmade hell brought forth by America's atomic capabilities, and *King Kong* (1933) had been re-released in 1953 for the film's 20th anniversary. The menagerie of metaphorical condemnations bludgeoned moviegoers with repetitive themes concerning our exploitation and negligence towards nature, reinforcing a message of morality.

Contrasting the tragic tale of Kong shot down from a skyscraper, Kronos cannot fall to its death, because Kronos *IS* a building. Frighteningly impersonal and abstract, the colossus constructed of cubes converts energy into matter, relentlessly consuming for its own benefit, regardless of the consequences. Panic ensues as the energy-leeching enigma ravishes the countryside, another example of our earned punishment for playing with power beyond our understanding. Unlike the immediate obliteration Godzilla leaves in its wake, the implications of an industrialized world drained of its technological power proves that, with Kronos' shameless snacking, the decimation of our planet goes out not with a bright bang, but with a slow descent into inoperative darkness.

Consumerism ran rampant in the 1950's as the country recovered from war, coinciding with an increased awareness of our reliance on Earth's finite natural resources, and the nation's curious affinity for watching movies featuring outsiders invading our turf. Extending the theme of "folks too detrimentally distracted by the seduction of scientific exploration to see what's right in front them" onto the characters in *Kronos*, even hottie heroine Vera gets overshadowed by her boyfriend's single-minded love affair with astronomy. Americans couldn't get enough... until the effects of overconsumption exposed an overlooked weakness that could be seen as a Pandora's Box of our own undoing.

Named after the power-hungry Greek god who devoured his children thought to be his rivals, *Kronos* symbolizes the destructive legacy we've left to ourselves, while acknowledging aspirations to further technological advancement. In a new age where vampiric AI sucks national electrical systems dry for the sake of photoshopping eight extra boobies onto Princess Leia, we should really consider the warning that our doomsday clock signals Earth is certainly ripe for the picking!

The Monolith Monsters

1957

PHOEF SUTTON

The 1950's was the time of giant monsters in America. Giant ants like *THEM!*. A giant octopus like *It Came From Beneath the Sea*. Giant people like *The Attack of the 50 Foot Woman*. And even, most horrifying, giant… rocks? Really? But no, these are not just any giant rocks. These are dark, crystalline, relentless, growing rocks that could destroy the world! Scared yet?

If not, you're a stronger person than I was as an eight-year-old, watching *The Monolith Monsters* on Channel 20 in Washington, DC. Face inches from the screen, I watched in rapt fascination as the rocks grew to enormous size, crashed to the ground and broke into shards, only to have each of those jagged fragments start to grow again in a never-ending cycle of destruction. I couldn't look away.

The movie begins, like so many sci-fi films of the day, with a view of the planet Earth. Mind you, this is a mid-century view of Earth, so the planet doesn't look the way it really does from space, shrouded in swirling clouds. No, no one had seen the Earth from afar yet, so here, our home world looks like a pristine globe, the kind you'd see sitting on

CINEMA BIZARRO

your teacher's desk at school.

And, over this, the voice of God tells us about meteors.

Or, if not the voice of God, the voice of Paul Frees, which is the next best thing. Frees was the voice-over artist extraordinaire of the post-War era. He gave vocal intonation to everyone from Ludwig Von Drake to Boris Badenov and even to the unseen "Ghost Host" of Disneyland's *Haunted Mansion* ride. If the Almighty did speak, you can bet He would sound like Paul Frees.

His lecture on meteors is illustrated by many images of craters and punctuated by a meteor sailing towards the screen (lifted from the same studio's earlier *It Came From Outer Space*, but effective all the same) and seeming to land in our lap. Only then do the opening credits start.

We find ourselves in the desert town of San Angelo, California. Local geologist, Ben (Phil Harvey) retrieves some pieces of the meteor from the crater. That night, the rocks surprise Ben by growing. Cue the music sting! The next morning, his partner Dave (Grant Williams) arrives at the laboratory to find the place torn apart and Ben turned to stone. The town doctor (Richard Cutting) is, understandably, puzzled by this. A local reporter, Martin (Les Tremayne) stops by the lab and is struck by the sheer number of black rocks scattered about the place. When he was there the day before, there was just one. What happened?

Meanwhile, the local schoolteacher, Cathy Barrett, takes her students on a desert field trip. One of the kids, little Ginny Simpson, picks up a piece of meteor and brings it home to her mother. The teacher is played (with a breathy sultriness that seems rather inappropriate) by the beautiful Lola Albright, just about to start a three-year run as *Peter Gunn*'s songstress in the private eye series.

Cathy and Dave go to the Simpson farm, which they find destroyed and under a pile of black rocks. Ginny's parents are dead, and Ginny is catatonic. They rush her to Dr. Steve Hendricks (Harry Jackson) at the California Medical Research Institute. He reports that Ginny is turning to stone! (The California Medical Research Institute, by the way, is the same facility that examined Grant Williams in *The Incredible Shrinking Man*. They weren't able to be of much help to him either.)

Slowly, they realize that these rocks are fragments of the meteorite

THE MONOLITH MONSTERS

and that when a person comes in contact with them, they turn to stone. By accident, Dave discovers that it is water that makes the stones propagate. Then, as if on cue, they realize that a major rainstorm is now falling. Racing to the site where the meteor fell, they see the black rocks growing into immensely tall "monoliths" that collapse, breaking into fragments. Each piece then repeats that cycle, on and on. They realize that from here the "monoliths" could spread and threaten all life on Earth.

It's at this point that this fairly predictable programmer rises to the level of a "Must-See" movie. Let's face it, the special effects are where most '50's sci-fi films let us down. They range from the ridiculous (the googly-eyed flying turkey from *The Giant Claw*), to the adequate (the huge puppet ants from *THEM!*), to the pretty-good-if-you-squint-a-little-bit (the enormous spider from *Tarantula*), to the totally sublime (Ray Harryhausen's stop-motion magic from *The Beast From 20,000 Fathoms*). But, all of them require some suspension of disbelief.

Indeed, I often feel sorry for the actors in these movies. While they are filming, they're usually acting with nothing, just a blank space, or maybe a stick with a ball on it. They have to hope that, when the movie is finished, the monster they're reacting to with such abject horror is a spectacular creature like Harryhausen's Ymir in *20 Million Miles to Earth* and not the *papier-mâché* dinosaurs from *Unknown Island*. They have no way of knowing whether they'll come out of it looking like good actors or fools.

The effects in *The Monolith Monsters* (from Universal's special effects department, who had done the stunning effects for *The Incredible Shrinking Man* that same year) are on an entirely different level. The masses of jet-black fragments grow to towering heights and crash down to split into pieces, littering the crater floor. Then, they grow from the rubble strewn on the ground; grow like jagged skyscrapers, reaching up to the air, then fall under their own weight to shatter again. And again, and again.

It's awesome. As a kid, I couldn't figure out how the special effects were done. Were they some crystalline organism, enlarged photographically? Even when I see it now, I'm mystified by the monoliths. I mean, I can tell they're miniatures, but still, the question remains: How the heck was this effect achieved? Now, Tom Weaver tells us that he heard from a special effects guru, who heard it from an old timer, who worked on the picture that the monoliths were made of… wood. That's right, plain old, ordinary balsa wood. Carved into jagged shapes, painted black and scored in spots so that they would break apart just as desired and filmed in slow motion. Voila!

Perhaps that's how they did it. But I don't really want to believe it. I prefer to believe they are real meteor bits, growing and growing and growing, because there's something about the absurdity of them being alien rocks – the very quality that people laughed about when the film came out – that makes the monoliths seem all the more frightening. They aren't sentient beings; they don't want to conquer the earth or enslave us. They are just rocks. Rocks that grow and destroy without any goal. Just because that's what they do. In time, Dave and the others discover that salt can destroy the monoliths. So, if they blow up the nearby dam and let it flood the local salt flats, the rushing flow of salt water will destroy the monoliths. And it works. They save the day. Just in time.

The Monolith Monsters is a good film, well-acted and competently written. The cinematography (by Ellis Carter) is evocative and the music score (uncredited, but composed by the usual Universal-International team of Irving Gertz, Henry Mancini and Herman Stein) is terrific.

But it's the monoliths themselves that make this picture so memorable. For once, the tag line that screamed across the top of the poster was an understatement: MAMMOTH SKYSCRAPERS OF STONE THUNDERING ACROSS THE EARTH!

Truer words were never spoken!

Quatermass 2

(US Title: ENEMY FROM SPACE) **1957**

STEVEN PEROS

Before Hammer Films' big screen adaptation of Nigel Kneale's 1953 hit, six-part, serialized, BBC TV production of *The Quatermass Experiment* appeared in movie theaters in 1955 as *The Quatermass Xperiment*, Hammer Films was already contemplating a sequel. BBC staff writer Kneale had not yet written a second Quatermass BBC serial so there was no TV show Hammer could adapt. Furthermore, Kneale was still under contract to the BBC, so when asked by Hammer for his permission to allow another writer to author a Quatermass feature film, he refused them, especially since he was unhappy with (a) Hammer's casting of gruff American actor Brian Donlevy as Quatermass and (b) BBC's shabby handling of his sharing in the profits of the financially successful film adaptation.

Hammer remained undeterred and instead made *X... the Unknown* (1956) to capitalize on *The Quatermass Xperiment*'s success. American actor Dean Jagger played the Quatermass-esque atomic scientist, Dr. Adam Royston, who finds an enemy from within the Earth rather than from outer space. It's a solid film, notable as the first feature screenwriting credit for a young Hammer Assistant Director named Jimmy Sangster, who would go on to help solidify the Hammer gothic horror brand with his screenplays for *Curse of Frankenstein* (1957) and *Horror of Dracula* (1958). It all went off without a hitch and Hammer had another adults-only sci-fi/horror hit on their hands.

While *X... the Unknown* was in production, Kneale wrote his second six-part Quatermass program for the BBC, *Quatermass 2*, which was broadcast in the Fall of 1955 and was a hit. When Hammer secured the film rights, Kneale took the opportunity to leave his staff position at the BBC and wrote the feature screenplay version himself, on which he shares writing credit with director Val Guest.

Much to Kneale's consternation, Brian Donlevy was once again cast as Professor Bernard Quatermass, the head of the British Experimental Rocket Group (with no one asking in either film why an American was appointed to such a high-ranking position within the British government). Of the three Quatermass films produced by Hammer, *Quatermass 2* (or *Quatermass II* depending on the poster art) was Kneale's most overtly political, using the sci-fi/horror arena to criticize the UK's dangerous, government-endorsed policy of unchecked secrecy and its potential for public peril.

When we come upon Quatermass, he has been denied funding by the government for the domed moon colony he has designed. However, when he and his assistant Marsh (Bryan Forbes) drive out to rural Wynderden Flats to investigate small, meteor-type objects landing in the countryside, he is shocked to see that a replica of his domed city has been built in the middle of nowhere.

When Marsh investigates one of the small, football-sized meteors, it cracks in his hands, emitting a gas which scars his face, leaving a "V" mark. Within moments, uniformed armed guards appear, all sporting a similar "V" on their faces or hands. Quatermass pleads with them, but the unconscious Marsh is whisked away.

Quatermass finds out that the installation is top secret and authorized by the government. He tries to explain to his higher-ups that what they think is going on there (the development of synthetic food) may not be what it seems. But the more he tells them about "V" markings and guards behaving like robots, the more he is dismissed as letting his imagination run away with itself. Standing his ground, Quatermass believes there is some alien presence at work, systematically taking over the minds and bodies of everyone from soldiers to possibly higher-ups in the government.

He finds a like-minded ally in a similarly suspicious Parliament member, Broadhead (Tom Chatto), who uses his influence to organize a tour of the secret synthetic food facility for himself, Quatermass, and a few others. Broadhead breaks away from the tour leader to investigate while Quatermass narrowly escapes a group alien take-over. In the film's most gruesome image, Quatermass finds Broadhead descending the steps from one of the domes. Turns out they do not house synthetic food but a black, burning, tar-like substance (which covers the dying Broadhead from head to foot).

Quatermass grabs a vehicle and flees the compound. Back in London, he takes his case to his old colleague from *The Quatermass Xperiment*, Inspector Lomax of Scotland Yard (played this time by John Longdon) demanding he get Scotland Yard to seize control of the facility. But when Lomax meets with his superior for permission to enter the top-secret facility, he takes pause when he sees the same "V" mark on the superior's wrist. Lomax wisely says nothing about Quatermass and his claims.

Quatermass enlists the aid of a newspaper reporter (Sidney James) to break the story. The reporter insists on first seeing it for himself. When they stop at the nearby village pub, the locals (yet to be marked by a "V") are very suspicious and fearful of the installation. While in the pub, more of the mini meteorites descend from above (turns out these all carry aliens in gaseous form), crashing inside the pub and leaving their "V" mark on some locals. The same V-marked alien guards, who the villagers call "zombies", storm the pub and execute the reporter as he is phoning in his story.

Quatermass and Lomax slip out, with Quatermass heading off to the compound solo while Lomax leads the enraged, armed villagers, hot on Quatermass's heels. The incognito Quatermass (sporting a uniform stolen from a fallen zombie soldier) discovers the horrible truth of what is housed at this compound, later explaining to the villagers: "Inside those domes are creatures from outside this earth. Thousands of tiny creatures that can join together and expand into a thing a hundred feet high! And each one can infect a human being. Those wretched creatures you call zombies... Take a look at them and you can find the mark!" He further explains that the mini-alien craft (in the form of meteorites) are descending from an alien mother asteroid that is hovering above the

CINEMA BIZARRO

earth (not unlike the conceit posed over three decades later in *Independence Day*)

Lomax and the armed villagers successfully storm the compound and join forces with Quatermass in the now sealed-off pressure control room where Quatermass turns a few dials, hoping to slowly suffocate the alien mass. The impatient village leaders decide they don't believe Quatermass, so they accept an offer from the zombie soldiers to be escorted to the dome to "see for themselves" that there's no such alien. As expected, the villagers are betrayed; their very bodies used as a form of corking to stop Quatermass's oxygen drain scheme, leading to perhaps British cinema's most disgusting image in one line as Quatermass explains of a newly blood-dripping pipe: "That pipe has been blocked with human pulp!"

Quatermass and company riddle the dome with bullets, exploding it and unleashing British cinema's first *kaiju*: three 200-foot-tall alien monster blobs. As Quatermass and Lomax escape, a rocket unleashed by his Rocket Group blows up the all-controlling asteroid, causing the three alien *kaiju* to instantly die and all the V-marked zombies to return to their former selves. Despite the seeming victory, the always suspect (and never sentimental) Quatermass can't help but wonder if we haven't seen the last of this alien menace.

Quatermass 2 is a solid, and more action-packed, follow-up to the excellent earlier film, bringing out the best in Hammer's resident composer, James Bernard. Guest makes great use of the Shell Haven Refinery in Essex, England, and the resultant giant globs from space do not disappoint, which is not usually the case. Hammer's international success with Dracula and Frankenstein came immediately after, putting future Quatermass films on hold until the third and final Hammer entry ten years later, *Quatermass and the Pit* (covered by this writer in *Giant Bug Cinema*), the best of an excellent trilogy.

THE BLOB

1958

DAN MADIGAN

Not many horror films from the 50's can boast that the lead of the picture would become a bona fide mega Hollywood superstar. *The Blob* could proudly wear that claim on its sleeve (if this transmogrifying monstrosity opted to wear clothes)

Our story opens when a romantic interlude on Lover's Lane, Small Town USA, is interrupted by a fiery meteorite crashing into a nearby forest, putting an abrupt halt to the amorous activities of a pair of teenage lovebirds. The twenty-eight-year-old Steve McQueen plays teenager Steve Andrews and his onscreen romantic partner, Jane Martin, is played by actress Aneta Corsaut (who would leave the world of movies and settle nicely into television, landing a role as Sheriff Taylor's girlfriend Helen Crump on *The Andy Griffith Show*. Corsaut wouldn't return to the world of horror until having a role in Dennis Donnelly's *Tool Box Murders* in 1977.)

But for McQueen, even in this humblest of beginnings, viewers could glimpse in him the charisma that would eventually lead him to his own western television series later that same year, *Wanted: Dead or Alive*, and then onto a storied career where he would become one of Hollywood's most sought after leading men.

    Realizing that a night of planned hanky-panky has been thwarted by an extemporaneous adventure of searching for the downed meteorite, Steve and Jane rush to find the crash site, only to find out they were beaten there by the town drunkard and soon-to-be sacrificial first kill Barney (played by Olin Howland, who is credited in this film as Olin Howlin, a prolific character actor who had a similar role a few years earlier in the groundbreaking *THEM!*). So, what does this inquisitive inebriate do when he sees this pulsating, unknown entity come slithering from inside of a still smoldering meteorite? Why, he prods it with a stick! What else would you do (besides leave it alone and get the hell out of there.)? Well, it's not long before the title creature decides to latch on to Barney and never let go. In fact, *The Blob* has a nasty habit of attaching itself to people and absorbing every one of them, leaving nothing behind (like some relatives we all know).

    So starts one of the most iconic horror films from the 1950's, a film that is the product of fusing two popular cinematic genres of the day, the Juvenile Delinquent film and the Horror movie. *The Blob* comes in the middle of the "teenagers vs monsters" cycle of films… somewhere between the teensploitation titles, *I Was a Teenage Werewolf*, *Invasion of the Saucer Men*, *The Blood of Dracula*, and *The Giant Gila Monster*. The themes of misunderstood teenagers battling adolescent angst, social isolation, disapproving parents, and disbelieving figures of authority creates an "us against them" vibe to the story, with the teens becoming the de facto heroes solely because no one over the age of thirty can relate to them nor take any credence in what they swear they've seen. It's a case of The Boy Who Cried Blob with no one but their peers initially going along with Steve and Jane's eyewitness claims that The Blob is both incredibly insatiable and seemingly indestructible. It's basically an intergalactic, gluttonous jello-shot with a penchant for human flesh.

    In the 1950's, our planet was a popular place for outer space visitors to just drop in for an impromptu visit or a well-planned-out invasion. The interplanetary interlopers came in all shapes and sizes, from the handsomely eloquent, human-like Micheal Rennie from *The Day the Earth Stood Still*, to the curvaceous leotard-clad Shirley Kilpatrick from

THE BLOB

The Astounding She-Monster, to the bi-ped, tri-eyed Martians in *War of the Worlds*, to the gigantic space-seedpods from *Invasion of the Body Snatchers*. The shapes have all been different, yet consistent, but what makes *The Blob*'s menacing more unpredictable is that every time it feeds, it grows. And this gelatinous glob of goo is always hungry.

But what happens if you can't stop this ravenous, cherry-red, all-consuming abomination? The usual good ol' standby of fire has no effect on the Blob. It isn't phased by electricity (which was good enough to destroy the horrific invader from *The Thing from Another World*), and since shooting it is futile, the most practical plan of attack is fleeing in panic-stricken terror. It's a serious question that needs a more serious solution. But a frosty *deus ex machina* late in the fourth quarter gives our heroes the go-ahead score that negates the Blob's goal into turning the world into a big, all-you-can-devour buffet. And no screen monster's death scene better addresses the dangers of climate change and its devastating thawing effect on mankind.

With one of the catchiest opening credit songs of any sci-fi movie (second only to *The Green Slime*, discussed elsewhere by me in this book) the single "Beware of the Blob" became a somewhat modest hit, reaching the Number 33 spot on The Billboard Hot 100. Sung by a group of studio musicians who came together as The Five Blobs (with lead vocals by singer/actor Bernie Knee) they managed to have a short career, but the impressive part of this song's origin is that it was penned by the multi Oscar-nominated Mack David and the legendary songwriter/composer Burt Bacharach (yes, that Burt Bacharach)! The two men would part ways, resulting in Bacharach partnering with Mack's younger brother, Hal David, on a meteoric string of hit songs.

The story concept was created by Irvine H. Millgate, then handed off to be written by Theodore Simonson (who would work with Yeaworth the next year on *The 4D Man*) and former actress Kay Linaker (who wrote screenplays under the *monster de plum* Kate Philips). Linaker had a very prolific acting career in films from 1936 to 1945, but mostly with bit roles, often uncredited. It is Linaker who is credited for coming up with the title, *The Blob*, after it first being called *The Molten Meteor*, then briefly (and thankfully not permanently), *The Glob*.

The Blob is the first film produced by Jack H. Harris, whose career as both a film financier and distributor would later help launch the careers of fledgling filmmakers John Landis (1973's *Schlock*) and director John Carpenter and writer Dan O'Bannon's first film *Dark Star* (1974).

The Blob was an independent film, one made outside of the Hollywood system and not held under the same duress-causing microscope that most studio-financed directors had to suffer under. Director Irvin Yeaworth had helmed a low-budget "juvenile delinquent film" the year before called *The Flaming Teen Age* and, keeping with the idea of working with mostly nonprofessional young actors, filled the cast of *The Blob* with many of them. Yeaworth continued his collaboration with Harris on two more sci-fi films: *The 4D Man* (1959) and *Dinosaurus!* (1960), and he would ultimately return to a filmic output of small movies based on religious, educational material, but *The Blob* stands out as his masterpiece. So forget the snobbish cinematic critics and the trolling detractors, *The Blob* is essential viewing for any horror/sci-fi fan.

In 1972, *Beware! The Blob* (aka *The Son of The Blob*), directed by actor Larry Hagman of TV's *I Dream of Jeannie*, hit the theaters. Hagman's only feature as a director (he directed episodes of *Jeannie* and later, *Dallas*), it is a sequel more comedic than its horrific predecessor, boasting an impressive cast, all of whom seem to be in on the joke. Thirty years after the original *The Blob* was released, Chuck Russell's solid remake of the same name debuted. With a fantastic plot twist and top-notch special effects, it makes for a worthy follow up to the original.

THE BRAIN FROM PLANET AROUS

1957

MIKE PEROS

The late 1950's saw a preponderance of alien invader films, many of which are covered in this volume. Some of these aliens are invisible, taking over people's bodies but without any discernible form of their own (I write about these kinds of invaders in 1959's *Invisible Invaders*, a few chapters down. You won't want to miss it.). Others can be seen, but mainly reside in the body of a hapless character. One of the more enduring examples is *The Brain from Planet Arous*, a sci-fi film from 1957 starring John Agar and directed by Nathan Juran, though you won't see Juran's name in the credits (more on that later).

Agar became a staple of these low-budget, late 1950's/early 1960's sci-fi funfests, which might be seen as a comedown after his 1940's efforts such as *Fort Apache* (1948), *She Wore a Yellow Ribbon* (1949) and *Sands of Iwo Jima* (1949). In these earlier films, directed by the likes of John Ford and Allan Dwan, and starring John Wayne (who would remain a friend and employer of Agar's), Agar projected sincerity, integrity, and naiveté. He had also married *Fort Apache* co-star and former child star

CINEMA BIZARRO

Shirley Temple, so it seemed easy street was within his grasp. Alas, the storybook union soon dissolved, Agar's career faltered (in part, because of his drinking), and he found himself cast in "B" films. While Agar was good as an honest, conflicted detective opposite Edmund O'Brien's corrupt and murderous cop in 1954's *Shield for Murder*, his 1950's efforts were mainly leads in either "B" Westerns or in Sci-Fi. And there were many of them, including 1955's *Revenge of the Creature* and *Tarantula*, 1956's *The Mole People*, and 1957's *The Daughter of Dr. Jekyll*. Depending on the movie, Agar would generally be an earnest scientist or a heroic (and earnest) army officer.

These roles weren't too complex, and Agar capably handled them. 1957's *The Brain from Planet Arous* was indeed something else. Here, Agar would be playing both hero and villain, as an esteemed nuclear scientist who runs afoul of an alien outlaw who takes over his body.

Agar's Steve March is engaged to Joyce Meadows' Sally Fulton, and all is blissful until March and Sally's brother Dan (Robert Fuller) do some cave exploring and are subjected to a blistering assault by a nefarious, if ephemeral, brain-shaped creature. March survives (barely) and returns home; though outwardly ok, he's been taken over by Gor, a fugitive, loquacious alien brute from the planet Arous. In the right hands, this role might have allowed an actor to deliver a memorable, even nuanced performance. While Agar doesn't quite have those chops, his efforts are always entertaining.

In his first scenes, Steve March is the Agar most film fans know, sincere and determined, tentatively affectionate toward his fiancé. After the alien encounter, Agar plays the inhabited Steve as a sleazy, smarmy, game show host who's only in it to kiss the female contestants. It only takes Sally one overly amorous, aggressive kiss to recognize something is amiss, yet she doesn't understand why. All she suspects is that it has something to do with the trip, especially when Marsh says that her devoted brother left for Vegas. Steve maintains "I'm still the same lovable character," but when her dog tries to protect Sally from Steve during an unsolicited advance, Steve throttles it, which further fuels Sally's feelings of unease.

The mystery of Gor's intentions is cleared up when Gor materializes at Steve's home in the form of a floating, two-eyed brain. Gor has plans for world domination and needs to reside inside Steve's body, both for his access to scientists and government leaders, and as a "dwelling place." In addition, since Gor is an alien with needs, he informs Steve (and the audience) that he plans on using Steve's body to put the moves on Sally. After Sally's concerned father arrives, there is an effective shot of a distorted, tormented Steve, unseen by the others, as viewed through the water cooler. Again, Steve attests that all is fine—but his now-deformed eyes, like Ray Milland's in *X, the Man with X-Ray Eyes* (1963), say otherwise.

Father and Sally go to the cave and find her brother's burned body, where they, too, are visited by another alien big brain from Arous in the form of Vol, who sounds a lot like Gor (understandable, since actor Dale Tate voices both). Unlike Gor, Vol is a "good brain" who takes them into his confidence and tells them of Gor's evil intentions. According to Vol, the only way to save humanity (and Steve) is to force the brain out of Steve's body. Meanwhile, Steve, behaving as a precursor to telekinetic Richard Burton in *The Medusa Touch* (1978), fixes his evil stare on an airborne passenger plane and wills it to explode, followed by an extreme close-up of a diabolically smiling Agar.

In order to keep an eye on Steve, Vol inhabits the dog's body, while the "five" of them (dog/Vol, Sally and Steve/Gor) go on a crowded date to a nearby lovers' lane. There, Steve lets Sally know about Gor's power, and together, they visit the scene of the plane crash, where Sally sees the victims have the same burns as her brother. From this point, the film becomes a series of scenes where Steve/Gor threatens and follows through. The sheriff wants to bring Steve in, but Steve/Gor stares him to death and laughs maniacally; Steve/Gor visits the site of some nuclear tests and tells the assembled brass they have to surrender to him or he will destroy the planet. When a general protests, Steve/Gor kills him (followed by that evil laugh—there are many evil laughs in this film). After he further demonstrates his powers by bringing down another plane, everyone is convinced of his capacity for doom.

Luckily for Steve (and for mankind), Gor needs to periodically leave Steve's body to get some air and survive, which allows Steve to bludgeon Gor to death in the precise spot intimated by a "how to" left by Sally. By the end, Vol and Gor are gone, the dog is back to being a

CINEMA BIZARRO

dog, and Steve still loves Sally, only without that extra frisson that Gor imbued him with. A mixed blessing, for sure.

Many people (myself included) are fond of this film—its director, Nathan Juran, was not. Juran was a studio veteran, having begun as an art director in the 1930s, racking up credits at 20th Century Fox (winning an Oscar for his work on 1941's *How Green Was My Valley*) and Universal, before turning to directing in the 1950's. His credits include Audie Murphy Westerns (like 1953's *Gunsmoke*) and a Rock Hudson swashbuckler (1953's *The Golden Blade*), but by the late 50's, Juran would be directing such sci-fi classics as *The Deadly Mantis* and *20 Million Miles to Earth* (both from 1957). Juran was unhappy with the way *Brain from Planet Arous* turned out. Perhaps it was because of the severe budget or "actor limitations" — whatever the reason, the pseudonym "Nathan Hertz" is on the credits. Yet *The Brain from Planet Arous* has its charms. It moves fairly well, though there are some static shots. The not-so-special effects reflect the shoe-string budget, but are fascinating in their own way. Agar is always watchable, particularly when Gor takes hold, and there are some interesting twists as the film goes on. What's more, you can easily stream it and discover its charms for yourself — or speculate as to why Juran disowned it.

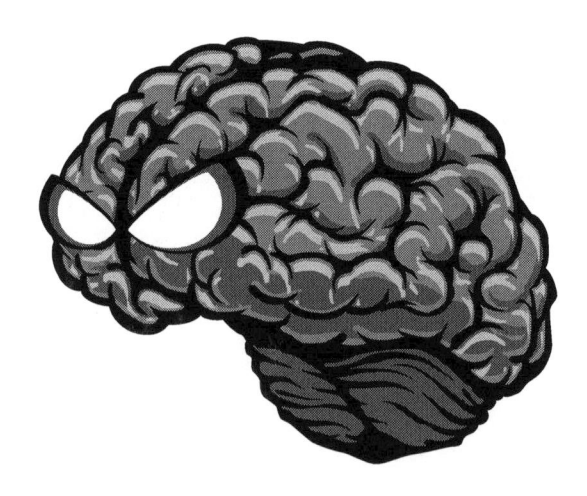

I MARRIED A MONSTER FROM OUTER SPACE

1958

LARRY BLAMIRE

I considered calling this chapter "The One with Valerie Allen" but thought better of it (more on that later). It's long been accepted that *I Married a Monster from Outer Space* is far better than its tabloid title might indicate, but I'm still not sure it's received its due. Subversive alien takeovers in 1950's films fall into two categories: 1) Inhabiting bodies, such as 1953's *Invaders from Mars*; or 2) Replacing them, as in 1956's *Invasion of the Body Snatchers*, and the final film of the cycle, 1963's small-scale *The Day Mars Invaded Earth*. *I Married a Monster from Outer Space* is fairly compact, with its experimental vanguard insinuating itself into American suburban serenity.

We are quickly introduced to a bunch of typical guys on a night out, celebrating Bill Farrell's (Tom Tryon) pending nuptials with the usual cheery hazing on the "horrors" of marriage. Bill leaves early, planning to check in on his bride-to-be, but doesn't make it, waylaid by a hideous alien (one of the best of the decade) who engulfs him in strange bubbling smoke. The following day, all are concerned he'll be late for the wedding, including Bill's bride, Marge (Gloria Talbott). But when he walks in at the last minute, we know Bill is no longer "Bill." This quickly leads to one of the most uncomfortable honeymoons in cinema history. Already, the subtext is writ large.

I Married a Monster from Outer Space's theme of traditional gender roles and marital challenges (not without sly amusement) is what keeps it from being a mere "rehash" of *Invasion of the Body Snatchers*. Just as the earlier film invited metaphors of communism and McCarthyism (Don Siegel's dismissals aside), so does *I Married a Monster from Outer Space* dare us to look intimately at outer space infiltration. *Mars Needs Women*, but why? The traditional "guy talk" of husbands complaining about "the old ball-and-chain" gets an interplanetary spin. The husbands are aliens to the wives, and the wives are aliens to the husbands. Whether intended or not, it's sometimes almost satirical and certainly unlike any other 1950's science fiction film. The concept of the *before and after* of marriage ("the honeymoon is over") now correlates with the before and after of alien possession. Sure, it's easy 'til the smoke bubbles.

If Val Lewton produced a space invasion movie, it might look something like this, most obviously because of Marge's eerie nighttime walk through suburb and wood as she follows Bill, hears a cat screech, then finds it dead (he already killed a puppy: a major no-no in 50's suburbia). But also, the paranoia-inducing downtown by night, where alien-possessed cops seem to pull up out of nowhere. Director Gene Fowler Jr. deserves some long overdue credit. There's nicely-jarring imagery: the insect walking on Tom Tryon's eye and those lightning flashes of alien faces beneath the human guise (kudos to effects great John Fulton for that and the nifty smoke effect). Those act as this movie's version of the telltale neck marks in *Invaders from Mars* or crooked pinkies in the TV series, *The Invaders*.

There's smart use of source music (jukeboxes, radios) in the opening, as we approach the night club, and later, in the dive bar scenes, giving us both a feeling of false security, yet also the expectation of something about to hit the fan. Max's bar, with its regulars, also suggests a safe haven from whatever unknown is out there, much like the café in Hitchcock's *The Birds*. Fowler and cinematographer Haskell Boggs stage and block these scenes nicely. Max himself (fighter turned actor "Slapsie Maxie" Rosenbloom), like Marge's raspy-voiced friend Helen

(Jean Carson), gives us reassurance that we're in the meat-and-potatoes real world. James Anderson's patented, shifty lowlife Weldon adds a welcome dynamic, with some choice brittle dialogue ("I never seen my grandmother."). His personal unpleasantness provides contrast to the very different discomfort the aliens emanate, and his inevitable confrontation with the false police bristles with energy and surprising brutality. Unsettling in a different way is Marge's scene with the police chief (John Eldredge) who happens to be her godfather. His fatherly concern manages to come off as both sincere and patronizing; as ominous in its own way as Bert Freed's icy police chief in *Invaders from Mars*.

"Bill isn't the man I fell in love with," says Marge in a twist on a typical soap opera. Gloria Talbott and Tom Tryon do convincing work navigating this ever-ratcheting relationship. Once Marge discovers Bill's an alien, screenwriter Louis Vittes pulls a brilliant reversal. Now it's Bill who remarks, "The past few weeks, you've changed… gone away." It gets even better after Sam and Helen's wedding when he confesses, "I think I'm way ahead on the deal… That wedding today… it meant something to me… I'm learning what love is." We are taken aback. Is this genuine? Is the alien feeling something?

More inspired writing from Vittes has Bill drowning his sorrow by not drinking (aliens can't) with fellow alien husbands Sam (Alan Dexter) and Harry (Robert Ivers), commiserating in very individual ways. Sam can't help but appreciate how Earth guys have a good time, while Harry finds the whole deal utterly disgusting, and Bill sulks, unsure how to process his newfound feeling. Later, they seem even more hapless as they cluelessly watch Sam drown.

"I seen a monster once," grins Francine provocatively as she floats up to the slimy Weldon at the bar, following Marge's distressed exit. I've had a big crush on Valerie Allen in this movie since I was a kid. As Francine ("the hooker," as she's usually labeled), she electrically charges every inch of screen. The beautiful and charismatic Allen had a busy acting career in a brief amount of time, mostly on television. She apparently had a lead in an Ernie Kovacs sitcom that ended with his untimely demise. *Leave it to Beaver* fans (present!) recall her as the woman who stiffed Beaver for the reward after he found her wallet. Allen later became an RCA executive, but her acting chops were undeniable

CINEMA BIZARRO

and her body language (a thing to behold) conveys so much about Francine and feels off-the-street real. She's always moderately intoxicated, with this slightly twitchy sashay (there's no other word). And Francine struts her stuff into, arguably, the most unforgettable scene in the film, thanks in large part to her, Fowler, Boggs and acclaimed editor George Tomasini, known for his work with Hitchcock. As Francine wanders out of the bar after the alien husbands leave, she spots a hooded figure across the street, staring in a shop window; a quietly unsettling sight in the dead of night, with no musical score. Naturally, she primes herself and crosses, moving in for the "kill." Her gradual approach of the figure is playful, teasing, pouty, a bite of the lip, eyes drifting closed as she struggles to focus. A brief insert reveals the hooded figure is staring at a child's doll. Finally, her bag of tricks, and patience, run out, and she swats the figure. When it turns, her look says it all. She runs but, bye-bye, Francine. The camera brings us back to the window, the monstrous face reflected beside the doll.

Marge's urging of the local doctor (Ken Lynch), and his brainstorm of rallying the town's dads (who can't be impotent aliens) into an armed posse, leads to a satisfying pitched battle in the woods and the strange sight of suspended bodies of victims who can now be revived. The impassive, unfeeling eradicators of mankind in those other invasion films have no arc like these guys. Lo and behold, as they drop one by one, we actually feel something for these orphans of cold space. Especially lovesick Bill, the last alien standing.

NIGHT OF THE Blood Beast

1958

LARRY BLAMIRE

"The first satellite creature to impregnate man with its chromosomes!" boldly declared the trailer. Like *Attack of the Crab Monsters* and *The Killer Shrews*, *Night of the Blood Beast* is a "compound movie." Small group, under siege, holed up in some isolated place (a mountain-top tracking station); a template for much sci-fi and horror to come. It opens like a cut-to-the-chase version of the following year's *First Man into Space*. In a scene intensely lit by *The Outer Limits* cinematographer John Nicholaus Jr., an experimental rocket piloted by John Corcoran (Michael Emmet) is struck by something and crash-lands, leaving the astronaut in a state resembling death. Worse, something hitched a ride.

Tightly directed by Bernard Kowalski, with an inventive script by Martin Varno, the tone of *Night of the Blood Beast* is serious, underplayed by a businesslike ensemble who form the film's collective protagonist: Dave (Ed Nelson, the only person I've ever heard pronounce Corcoran, cor-COR-an), Julie (Angela Greene) who's romantically involved with John, Steve (John Baer), Donna (Georgianna Carter, whose picture should be in the dictionary next to "winsome") and the oldest, Dr. Wyman (Tyler McVey). Let me just say that many were the Monster Kids disappointed that the giant creature-hand holding a severed human head in the poster was not in the movie. However, those same kids watching late night TV (like me) had no time to fret over such disingenuous advertising, since the film, as such, has a few jolts of its own.

"Seven hours and his blood is still alive," remarks Dr. Wyman, trying to fathom John's living-dead state. Things at the station get even stranger when power is cut and vehicles and radio cease to function. "We're in a magnetic force field," deduces Dave, "a net of static electricity surrounding the whole area," which he attributes to "a very powerful magnetic source somewhere nearby, reversing all positive electrical power." The first of several suspenseful scenes takes place when Dave goes outside to check the tower. He finds a ladder swinging ominously while, inside, lights begin flickering. So, when Dave turns his back to camera to lock a gate, we are already uneasy. Especially when we cut to the POV of something watching him from the trees, bushes parting in the foreground. This causes Dave to turn, taking out his sidearm. Back to the foreground trees; a dark mass rises, blotting Dave in the background. The creature's POV rushes Dave, who backs away shooting. As the others come running out, we hear an off-camera scream (obviously dubbed by someone other than Nelson). They no sooner confirm that Dave is okay when a crash comes from inside the building. This kind of piling-on of action comes unexpectedly, as we are used to a certain pacing in these films, where action is followed by a period of dialogue. This makes the audience ready for anything. So is the team, who now take a precaution that might have saved countless lives in future horror movies. They decide to stay in the same room.

The final shot of this sequence is unsettling: Dr. Wyman staying up, working at his desk, with the not-deceased body of John in the window behind him. But that doesn't prepare us for the film's most gruesome image. After a noise awakens everyone, we see Wyman's clipboard on the floor, blood dripping on it. Then, Dave and Steve staring at Wyman's dripping hands in the foreground with a further reveal of Wyman's body hanging upside down. Though it's facing away, Steve's shocker of a line tells all: "Half his head's gone." Strong stuff for 1958. It's like seeing what they couldn't show in *The Thing from Another World* earlier that decade. "Whatever it is, it works fast," observes Dave.

NIGHT OF THE BLOOD BEAST

Another potent setup from director Kowalski has Nicholaus framing Julie and Donna on either side of the lab window. A hand, in closeup, slowly rises into frame on the other side of the glass. Then, John, staring wildly (again, lit not unlike Nicholaus's *Outer Limits* work), struggles to pull himself up. Punch in close on John, whip pan to Donna, who turns and screams at camera. That is one crisp sequence.

The resurrected John is confused but spouts fluent science-speak, believing Wyman is now part of him. He then blurts, "It didn't come here to destroy!" referring to the creature, echoing the deluded philosophy of Lee Van Cleef's Dr. Tom Anderson in *It Conquered the World* (1956). The microscopic aliens observed earlier in his bloodstream are now, via fluoroscope, much larger; a notion made no less alarming by the fact they somewhat resemble sea monkeys. John is an alien breeding ground. "If you destroy them, you destroy me."

It should be noted that the film's only padding is a tendency to repeat dialogue, which does not detract from the whole, and in this case provides a hell of a punch. When John again states, "You can't destroy them," Steve asks, "Why not?" "*That's* why not," snaps John as we whip pan to the creature busting through the door. This erupts in a blazing gun-and-monster battle and our first good glimpse of the suit (modified from *Teenage Caveman*), whose bug eyes and beak have frankly grown on me over the years.

Comparisons with *It Conquered the World* are fairly obvious, but this creature distances itself by effectively communicating, whereas, in the end, the Venusian of the latter is just one more monster to kill. And John is more an impassioned victim than a brainwashed traitor, as Dr. Anderson comes off. In fact, thanks to John's self-doubting sincerity, we even wonder if he might be right. *Night of the Blood Beast* tips over the monster movie expectation that things that come from space need to be destroyed. Who can argue with heartfelt pleas for understanding and tolerance? Hell, the creature's race faced the same problem of atomic self-destruction that we face, circling earth for centuries, waiting for a serviceable projectile to gain entry. "You need me… and I have come," states the alien. Yet John wrestle with doubts; is it his own free will? Or the creature's suggestion of it?

While nobody actually says, "Try telling that to the missing half of

CINEMA BIZARRO

Wyman's head!" that's the general feeling. Nevertheless, they agree to meet with it. But Dave and Steve don't trust it and, knowing its susceptibility to fire, plot to betray John via Molotov cocktails. Normally, this would feel like good guys trying to save the day, but next to John's altruism, it comes off as petty ignorance in the face of the unknown.

The climactic meeting takes place at (where else?) Bronson Caves, where Kowalski, Nicholaus, and editor Jodie Copelan (*Night Tide*) pull off something special. As the creature finally speaks (McVey's voice, altered *Outer Limits* style), it echoes over a briskly cut montage of more camera setups than one would expect from a film of this budget (high angles, low, wide, wider) that elevates the material to something of far greater consequence. The alien explains the absconding of Wyman's brain tissue (enabling him to communicate) as a necessary sacrifice. But when the creature finally outlines its plan to unite all their intellects in one body, John says, "Check, please." He sees it as sacrificing his own civilization to resurrect theirs. "What you propose is dominance, not salvation." The creature responds amusingly (like a politician) with what sound like prepackaged comebacks ("Don't be governed by your fears.") and strangely calm rebuttals ("That's not true.")

John, certain he's saving mankind, sacrifices himself and the aliens growing within. As the creature is destroyed by fire, it warns, "You are not ready!" It seems mere chance that the betrayal by Steve and Dave just *happened* to be correct. Nevertheless, the team is left expressing mixed feelings, hoping they made the right decision.

INVISIBLE INVADERS

1959

MIKE PEROS

By the time *Invisible Invaders* was released, low-budget sci-fi films were all the rage in Hollywood (When you consider reviews at the time, one could almost take that literally). Some were successful almost immediately, while others raced toward obscurity, only to be rediscovered and achieve cult status years later. *Invisible Invaders* was one of those that didn't make the grade at first, with only a limited release on the bottom part of a double (or even triple) bill. There was some talent in front and behind the camera: Veteran director Edward L. Cahn's resume reached back to the *Our Gang* shorts of the late 1930's and early 1940's, and more recently, Cahn had directed *It! The Terror from Beyond Space*, which has been acknowledged as a major influence on Ridley Scott's *Alien*. Top-billed John Agar, a veteran of "B" horror/sci-fi films, had worked with Cahn the previous year in *Jet Attack*. Robert Hutton debuted in 1944's *Hollywood Canteen* and would later turn to directing (1963's *The Slime People*). Jean Byron was four years away from playing Patty Duke's Mom on *The Patty Duke Show*. The ubiquitous John Carradine, who would tally over three hundred credits, was also among the cast (see this writer's chapter on *Billy the Kid vs. Dracula*). Not exactly a group of lightweights.

The film starts with Carradine's character, noted atomic scientist, Dr. Karol Noymann, being blown up in a lab explosion. Noymann's colleague, Dr. Penner (Philip Tonge) resigns in the aftermath (Despite the prominence of John Agar in the credits, Philip Tonge has perhaps the main role. If you're a fan of classic films, you've seen Tonge many times, notably in *Miracle on 34th Street* as Maureen O'Hara's colleague, Mr. Shellhammer, and Billy Wilder's *Witness for the Prosecution* as Chief Inspector Hearne. This was his last major role.). While Dr. Penner grieves, Dr. Noymann appears at Penner's door, or more accurately, an invisible alien invader using Noymann's body to communicate (considering he was killed in a lab *explosion*, either Noymann's remains must have been pretty darn intact, or the mortician has done the best cosmetic job *ever*.) Noymann tells Penner the Earth must surrender within twenty-four hours to him and his fellow invisible invaders or else they will inhabit other dead bodies and cause mass destruction. Noymann declares, "We have never been defeated!" and informs Penner he's been chosen because his voice is among the loudest calling for peace. To seal the deal, Noymann hands Penner some strong material that becomes invisible (which is also used to camouflage their ships) and says, "You have had your warning!"

After Penner tells his daughter Phyllis (Jean Byron) and colleague Dr. Lamont (Robert Hutton) about the alien's doomsday threat, they're a little skeptical. But Penner persists and soon becomes *persona non grata* in scientific and military circles. After this humiliation, the three visit Noymann's grave, where they encounter an invisible alien (we know he's around because of some not-so-subtle tree jostling). The disembodied Noymann gives the earth one more warning, but this time, he backs it up with action: An alien in the body of a dead pilot goes to a hockey game (sounds like the opening to a joke), where he strangles the announcer and makes his own announcement, demanding that the Earth surrender (this never happens at Madison Square Garden.). Bedlam ensues, with invaders taking over the bodies of more dead people, and now we're transported to the land of montages and stock footage, with mass hysteria, fires, explosions, dam breaks, while Carradine's voice forcefully intones that the end is nigh.

Penner is finally taken seriously (the U.S. military obviously needed a brick to fall on its head) and he, Phyllis, and Lamont are escorted by

John Agar's Major Bruce Jay to a secret bunker. Jay has seen the horrors: "The walking dead are everywhere." When one sees all the footage of these inhabited dead bodies moving slowly and jerkily down hills, one can't help but note how this film influenced director George Romero and the zombies of *Night of the Living Dead* (1968).

While bunker-bound, they are waylaid by a desperate, gun-toting farmer (Hal Tomey) who tries to take their car; Agar's take-charge Major Jay shoots him dead, and an invisible invader (lying in wait) takes over the farmer's body (one can always spot an invisible invader through the re-use of earlier tree-jostling footage). At the bunker, there is some discussion about how to stop the aliens (ascertained to be radioactive), and how to make them visible. This invisibility seems to be the aliens' only strong suit, since any weapons they're using to destroy us are *ours* (We're so helpful.). They plan to capture an alien by using an acrylic spray that forms a hard, visible shell, with a worried Lamont emerging as the weak link among the bunker-hunkerers. A side note on the actor playing Lamont: Robert Hutton was a Warner Bros. romantic lead in the days when the major stars were off at war. Lest you think he'll wind up with Phyllis, remember that John Agar's strong, virile, better-billed Major Jay is on the scene.

While the first attempt at capturing an alien fails, the second time is a charm, as Jay and Lamont lure the farmer/alien (that dead farmer moves a helluva lot faster than those other dead bodies) to a pit filled with acrylic liquid. They get their alien, but soon, other invaders will come knock, knock, knocking on Penner's door. A few days of fruitless experiments go by and the alien (now out of its casing and using Carradine's voice) tells them to surrender… or else. Jay and Penner say "no way" but Lamont is not so sure. The narrator (an unbilled John Dehner) reminds us that with "every moment of failure, thousands more on earth would die!" Which is followed by even more narration and more stock footage of mass destruction.

By now Lamont wants to give up, so he and Jay have at it, inadvertently setting off a piercing alarm which causes the alien to go bonkers. Penner realizes that the way to handle an alien is with extremely loud sounds. As luck would have it, the multi-purpose bunker has all the tools needed to create a "sound gun" and kill the alien prisoner. However, the four can't share this vital intel with Washington because their radio is jammed by the nearby alien ship. They set out to find the jam source and kill a few plodding aliens along the way (that sound gun works). An alien shoots Major Jay, but he manages to silence both the aliens and the alien ship. Penner is able to get through to the military, while Phyllis tends to the wounded Major Jay. At the end, Penner, Lamont, Major Jay, and the (possibly) future Mrs. Major Jay receive thanks from a grateful nation, while the narrator assures us that this shows that "nations could work and come together in a common cause." Would that were true now.

As mentioned earlier, *Invisible Invaders* barely made a dent when first released, but has achieved cult status over time. It is compact (sixty-six minutes) and fast-moving. The acting is fine, and besides Philip Tonge's good work, John Agar is tough and confident as the Major, with some line readings having the "touch" of John Wayne. The film does address ideas regarding peace and the use of nuclear energy — the peaceful Penner is initially against nuclear energy but gravitates toward nuclear testing as a way of preserving peace, almost like a "reverse Oppenheimer." What hurts the film is a preponderance of not only stock footage, but narration. Narration can be a useful device, but here, the narrator is mostly telling us what we already know or, as in the "trap the alien" scene, what we can see all too clearly. But don't let my minor caveats keep you from seeing the immensely entertaining *Invisible Invaders*, as its unpretentious qualities are fairly visible.

THE CREEPING TERROR

1964

TRACY MERCER

The phrase "the worst film ever made" shows up a lot in our real world and in online conversations as a response to whatever is the latest over-budgeted Netflix original film starring – let's say, hypothetically – Jennifer Lopez or about the current, bloated DC attempt to get Superman or Aquaman right. Among film buffs and cinema historians, *Troll 2*, *The Room*, or *Plan 9 from Outer Space* historically all get the most shoutouts for being considered among "the worst" films ever made. Well, dear reader, I am here to refute ALL of those claims because clearly, the worst film ever made is 1964's *The Creeping Terror*. As such, this cult gem demands your attention as a worthy *Cinema Bizarro* movie and your consideration.

CINEMA BIZARRO

The story behind making *The Creeping Terror* with its infamous director is definitely more interesting than the film itself, but once you know the backstory, it makes viewing this cult classic even more entertaining. In fact, the behind-the-scenes insanity of this film is a jumping-off point for a 2014 indie film called *The Creep Behind the Camera*. Said real-life creep would be the director, who is credited on the 1964 film as Vic Savage. Savage was a pseudonym for real life baddie, A.J. 'Art' Nelson. A detailed look into Nelson's life reveals accusations including his being a con artist, wife beater, drug abuser, child porn peddler, and bigamist. Some accounts suggest he shot the actor who played Alfalfa on "The Little Rascals," ran afoul of mobster Mickey Cohen, may have stalked Mamie Van Doren, and was introduced to his *Creeping Terror* Assistant Director by Charles Manson. What Nelson shouldn't be mistaken for is being a credible motion picture director. I should also point out that his "Vic Savage" is credited as directing, producing, and editing the film in addition to being cast in the lead as Sheriff Deputy Martin.

Nelson's conman self knew credited writer Robert Silliphant and it was Robert's little brother, Allan who came up with the original concept for *The Creeping Terror*. You should know that their other brother, Stirling, was a highly regarded TV writer of the era, best known for writing on TV hits like *Route 66*, *Night Gallery*, and *Perry Mason*. Three years later, he would win an Oscar for writing *In the Heat of the Night*. Nelson used the Silliphant connection to sucker Hollywood investors to put money into his creature feature. Eventually, Allan left the production, realizing the film was rife with problems and could reflect badly on himself and his family. The picture was supposed to shoot in Lake Tahoe, but to save money, Nelson instead shot many of the film's pond sequences on Charles Manson's infamous Spawn Ranch compound in Simi Valley. After not paying the monster special effects creator, the artist stole his creature costume the night before filming was to begin. Undaunted, Nelson created a makeshift creature in the style of the purloined monster and the cameras started to roll!

You are wondering about the plot? The story is centered on the mayhem caused by cinema's slowest moving extraterrestrial creature (which resembles a floating blanket designed to look like a snail) after it lands its UFO in a small town and begins to eat people who seem to just ac-

CREEPING TERROR

cept their fate and allow themselves to be consumed by laying down and waiting to be overtaken. We are introduced to only the thinnest of sketched characters who mostly function to be eaten or make really poor choices about how to dispatch – again – THE SLOWEST moving ET in film history. The slug ET makes George Romero's *Night of the Living Dead*'s zombies seem like Olympian track and field medalists.

Our cast of characters: A newbie sheriff deputy (played by the director/scam artist behind the production), his newlywed wife, a bunch of military troops who only fire their guns at the stalking creature when huddled in a cluster, a scientist with no really good ideas, a few locals in dance halls, and teens who make out in cars. There is also a fisherman and his grandson who also wander aimlessly near slugo in a silly sequence that feels like it lasts for an hour.

In recent years, *The Creeping Terror* has found a following and that could be in part because of episode #606 of *Mystery Science Theater 3000*, which celebrates this movie to levels usually reserved for conversations about Ed Wood's work. I'm not convinced that Bela Lugosi's wrestling with a giant, fake octopus in Wood's 1955 classic, *Bride of the Monster* is any less or more professional than our slugo alien in Nelson's film. Perhaps also helping to create buzz for a revival of the film was Nelson's wife Lois' tell-all book about their life together. The book includes salacious details like when Nelson tried to introduce prostitutes into their relationship while she was suicidal – certainly, his real-life exploits were more shocking than anything he committed to celluloid.

Aside from the assuredly not scary creature (who, when he kills, usually does so to a jazz score!) and characters you never care about, what's most remarkable about this film is how little actual dialogue there is. There is some debate about what really happened regarding the audio tracks to the film. Some folks maintain the majority of dialogue was never actually recorded, others believe the audio tracks were too poor in quality to be used, while some crew members think the audio was just lost. As a result, the film is largely NARRATED by a disconnected voice, which means the audience is left watching foolish characters walk around in scenes as a narrator tells us what they are saying to each other – as characters' lips can be seen moving – or at other times, telling us what the characters are thinking. A fun factoid: Nelson hired Larry

CINEMA BIZARRO

Burrell, a local radio news anchor, to narrate the story in his best effort to cheaply cover for his lack of audio and inability to afford dubbing. Mr. Burrell has additional film credits to his name with the titles, *Not Tonight Henry* and *They Saved Hitler's Brain*.

This campy delight is packed full of endless scenes that all could have been cut in half, zero overall pacing, and one ridiculous kill after another. One of the most preposterous sequences involves an attempt to show a rocket ship landing that is clearly just a *launch* of a rocket ship played in reverse. This film also may be the first and last time a creature tried to have sex with a sportscar onscreen.

After production ended, more problems befell the film. It is believed that Nelson had a silent picture Moviola he used to roughly assemble the film while off the grid. Why did he vanish? Because he was a wanted man who was being sued by investors and was about to be indicted for fraud. Art Nelson, aka Vic Savage, was never to be seen again in film circles, and it was believed that he died of liver failure less than a decade after his would-be directing career creeped to an end.

The main financer, William Thourlby, acquired all the film elements he could find and paid to get another version edited with the hopes of selling it to drive-ins to recoup any money. He succeeded. Without Thourlby's efforts, we would never be able to enjoy the pure schlock that is *The Creeping Terror*. So, when you watch the film, look for the character of Dr Bradford and salute him – that's Thourlby's screen cameo and the man we truly have to thank for this camptastic gem existing.

DOGORA

1964/1966

BRIAN R. SOLOMON

Like its spiritual predecessor, *Gorath* (covered in *Giant Beast Cinema*), *Dogora* is another classic entry from the heyday of Japanese science fiction cinema in the 1960's, which also deals with a threat to Earth from outer space, and which also languished in obscurity for years. Unlike much more popular fare from the era like *Mothra* (1961), *Rodan* (1956) and of course the copious Godzilla films, *Dogora* flew relatively under the radar in the United States, and in fact did not receive a proper English-language home video release until the 21st century. In hindsight, it is fair to categorize it as one of the lesser Toho Studio efforts of the period, but it is nevertheless an ambitious film with much to recommend it.

Perhaps one of the reasons it did not connect with Western audiences (and distributors) is the fact that its titular monster, if it can even be called such, is difficult to define, and is hardly seen in the movie. Starting life as ambiguous "space cells" which are exposed to radiation in Earth's orbit, the unorthodox form of alien life first manifests itself as a giant protozoa, and it is only later that it appears in its giant jellyfish-like form, as it was advertised in marketing materials for the picture. And even then, it is really only in one scene, although it is an impressive one from a visual effects standpoint.

Despite its often-downplayed reputation in later years, the Toho Special Effects Department, headed up by Eiji Tsuburaya, was known for its ingenuity and cutting-edge techniques at the time. But *Dogora* represents one of the occasions on which their ambition may have exceeded their resources. Monster designer Keizo Murase, working off a unique 3-D design put together by illustrator Shigeru Komatsuzaki, crafted the monster using the then-new technique of soft-vinyl molding. It would be vastly different from other Japanese movie monsters, in that it was not a man in a suit, but rather a prop that had to be suspended on wires. Due to the fragility of the model, it was decided that it should be filmed while suspended in water. The extremely complicated nature of this process is the main reason that the monster is hardly seen in the film in its final form.

Thankfully, the movie doesn't really require the constant presence of the monster to move along at a brisk pace. With a script by Toho regular screenwriter, Shinichi Sekizawa, the same man responsible for such work as *Varan the Unbelievable* (1958), *Battle in Outer Space* (1959), *King Kong vs. Godzilla* (1962) and *Atragon* (1963), the story combines science fiction with gangster action and even international spy intrigue in a way that, although not always seamless, does keep the viewer engaged, for the most part. Originally pitched in 1962 as a futuristic epic in the same mold as *Gorath*, the project languished in developmental hell for two years until Sekizawa was brought in to tackle the original concept, scaling things back to set the picture in modern times, perhaps as a nod to budget limitations.

Under the direction of Toho's supreme workman, Ishiro Honda, the movie blends different genres in an unusual way. Because Dogora requires carbon to survive, it begins siphoning coal from the Earth's surface. More importantly, it begins absorbing diamonds, which causes it to unwittingly run afoul of a cartel of jewel-thieving gangsters whose plans are thwarted when the gems they're hauling suddenly vanish. The gangster subplot also allows the film to veer in other directions, away from the science fiction elements entirely at times, which again may have been an attempt to distract from the special effects difficulties, and at times can make the film a challenge for those who are expecting more of a traditional giant monster movie.

The movie is nothing if not imaginative, with well-executed action sequences and an interesting method of foiling the creature that involves the use of mass-produced, synthetic wasp venom, revealed to be Dogora's ultimate weakness for reasons that are really not all that important. The monster action set pieces, although few and far between, never fail to engage, with Murase and his supervisor, Tsuburaya, making the best of what they had to work with, with surprisingly impressive results.

The most endearing element of the human side of the picture comes from the presence of American actor Robert Dunham, who steals the show as Mark Jackson, the mysterious and much-talked-about adversary of the gangster cartel, who is later revealed to be a secret agent investigating the diamond heists. Dunham, whose residence in Japan during the golden age of Japanese genre cinema caused him to pop up in several films of the period, speaks all his lines in perfect Japanese and has an undeniable charm that anchors the film whenever he's on screen.

In fact, Toho was reportedly so pleased with Dunham's performance, they had partially planned for *Dogora* to be the launching point for a whole series of films centered on the Jackson character. Dunham would even explain in later years that the studio sent him to Hollywood to try to negotiate a distribution deal for their concept, but unfortunately, the plans would be shot down when American distributors complained that Dunham's dubbed-English performance (recorded by a different actor) made it impossible to gauge his acting abilities. They also complained that Dunham was not a well-known actor in America, which Dunham would insist was the reason that the much-more renowned Nick Adams would be used instead of him in later Toho films, though Dunham would famously appear again as the Seatopian Emperor in *Godzilla vs. Megalon* (1973).

Dogora was released to Japanese cinemas in the summer of 1964 under the full title of *Uchu Daikaiju Dogora*, which translates to *Giant Space Monster Dogora*. But without a major star or a conventional monster to anchor it, the movie didn't make it into American theaters.

CINEMA BIZARRO

As with *Matango*, it would be sold to the television distribution wing of American International Pictures, which brought it to U.S. TV in 1966 under the name *Dogora, the Space Monster*. It became one of the lesser entries in late-night B-movie syndicated TV, but nevertheless made an impression at the time among the "monster kids" who were lucky enough to catch it. It even made its way into an episode of the 1970's Norman Lear sitcom, *Sanford & Son*, when the main character Fred Sanford (played by Red Foxx) references the movie (similarly to how Carroll O'Connor's Archie Bunker would later reference Godzilla in an episode of *Archie Bunker's Place*, another Lear sitcom).

Sadly, *Dogora* completely skipped over the VHS B-movie craze of the 1980's and 1990's, and after its TV run in the 1960's and 1970's, was all-but-forgotten in the United States until Media Blasters finally gave it the deluxe DVD treatment in the summer of 2005, using the original Japanese version as well as the English-language dub that was created for the American television release. Although its profile has most certainly been raised in the past 20 years among lovers of classic science fiction cinema, it has never quite broken through into the pantheon of universally praised Toho masterpieces of the era. And yet, it continues to be discovered by completists and all those curious about international genre cinema, especially the films that don't perfectly fit the accepted Japanese monster-movie mold.

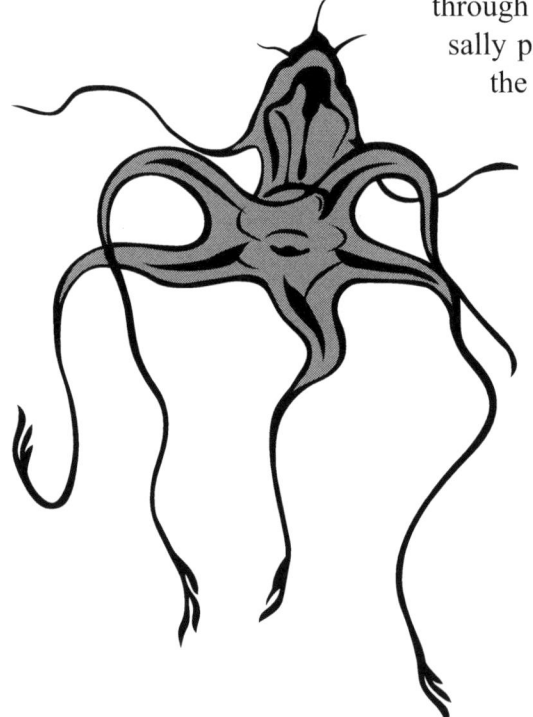

THE BUBBLE

1966

NADIA ROBERTSON

Television has always posed a threat to the theatrical experience. Replacing radio as the main medium of broadcast entertainment during the 1940's, television dominated households within a decade, causing a downfall in theater admissions by nearly 50% of previous attendance. Desperate to fill seats, studios began a renaissance of 3D motion pictures that would denote the 1950's as an era responsible for reinstating the popularity of stereoscopic, silver screen spectacles. Answering the call to revive a struggling theatrical landscape, Arch Oboler's *The Bubble* ushered in a new age for audiences ready to return to the exhilarating thrills only the big screen could offer.

Arch Oboler was a pioneer of pulp fiction and a renaissance man in his own right, an interesting fella who committed to carrying a piece of meteor in his pocket because the idea of other worlds intrigued him. An artist exhibiting an enthusiasm for creating sensational stories across all areas of show biz, Oboler (first known in the 1930's for his radio plays) aspired to achieve renown similar to that of his airwave idol, Orson Welles. Facilitating the entertainment industry's fascination with special effects extravaganzas, Oboler introduced to the world the very first 3D, feature-length, color film (*Bwana Devil* - 1952), creating a craze for

CINEMA BIZARRO

the format throughout the 50's that would help salvage poorly attended cinemas. The film featured a dual-strip, polarized process that would be further polished later to present a new way of watching movies in widescreen: "Space Vision". This improved screening system fostered the development of the single strip, three-dimensional technology still used to this day, first showcased in *The Bubble*.

Oboler shopping the script around to major studios proved unsuccessful. Fortunately, his resume in radio came to the rescue when Capitol Records stepped in to independently finance the film, allowing the artist to retain creative control of his project.

The Bubble begins with Mark (Michael Cole of TV's *The Mod Squad*) and his wife, Catherine (Deborah Walley) stuck inside a small airplane as she battles breaching their incoming infant midair while their pilot, Tony (radio star, Johnny Desmond) weathers a safe landing amid a turbulent storm. After touching ground, the couple make it to a hospital where Mark checks in on his wife and baby before venturing out into town. What he sees there is weird: a mishmash of studio backlots smashed together with a town square whose occupants have been hypnotized into living automatons. At this point, he's probably regretting taking his nine-month pregnant partner on that plane ride.

Observing these mindless zombies, it's clear the lights are on, but nobody's home. Ensnared in an endless cycle of menial movement, they are powerless to the ever-watchful master secretly pulling the strings from the skies. A structure resembling a termite colony in the center of the city requires residents to enter and exit like hive-mind insects to "recharge" at "The Station" - a pod that ensures people remain like bugs trapped under a jar, entranced in a state of ignorant repetition. Unable to enjoy life, they simply go through the motions, helplessly imprisoned by the curse of impassiveness caused by the unseeable creator of this chaos. The subject of the undead and alive alike returning to the comforts of the familiar in George Romero's *Dawn of the Dead* (1978) share a similar condemnation of the constraints of consumerism with Oboler's *The Bubble*, which was released over a decade before.

Some see *The Bubble*'s narrative structure to be meandering and meaningless, a lackluster script lost in a sea of unanswered enigmas and continuity conundrums. This is due to several factors, including Oboler cutting down the runtime to address criticisms of length, as well as the film being found in poor condition prior to its restoration (spearheaded by archivist Bob Furmanek for the Kino Classics release in 2014). Although the missing elements arguably make the film feel cobbled together, the resulting discombobulation complements the confusion experienced by the characters, positioning the audience to be bewildered alongside the protagonists.

Perhaps the script proselytizes profundity in its grandiose speeches; Oboler's affinity for exploring existentialism in the face of an unknown universe seeps into his sci-fi stories. A practitioner of metatextuality within his works, Oboler positioned the audience to observe his characters living within the screen as they are trapped inside a "bubble" conceived and cultivated by an observational alien architect. Placing the viewer in the same point of view as the story's antagonistic observer, Oboler applied a self-aware approach to *The Bubble* in order to turn a lens on the voyeurism inherent in the cinematic experience. The intentional ambiguity of a cruel overlord captor plucking people away when they prove to be a nuisance, alongside the film's deep dive into concepts of constricting free will within a heavily surveilled society, directly challenges compassionless capitalist constructs that prioritize production and profits over the quality of its citizens' wellbeing.

Arch Oboler's films tackled topics of autonomy and individualism during a time when the world was pushing back against the status quo. The 1950's became notorious for mass-marketed materialism, conflating the concept of personal success and happiness with excessive spending on commercial commodities. By the 1960's, popular artists across artistic mediums vocalized their dissent with anti-establishment sentiments. Coincidently, Disney had opened the gates to its kingdom in 1955, including Tomorrowland, with Walt Disney's utopian vision of the future where man and machine productively coexist. What became a worshipped place where "dreams come true" could simultaneously be interpreted as a power-hungry corporation creating a highly curated and controlled fantasy world built to exploit the connection between emotional dependence on purchasing stuff linked to self-satisfaction. Shocked into a stupor, placated people stay willfully surrounded by a make-believe place operating outside normal space and time. Released 10 years afterward, *The Bubble* could reflect a plea to break free from

CINEMA BIZARRO

a conditioned obedience to an ambivalent higher power manipulating a purposefully dazed public.

In today's times, streaming services and social media apps cast the same shadow on theaters as did the dawn of television, causing concern for cinephiles contemplating cinema's death knell. Silenced into submission by a fixation on escapism through entertainment, society has surrounded itself in its own bubble as we remain blissfully unaware of the forces that dictate our values. Values born from a fantasy maintained by Hollywood, the land of the most infamous facade. *The Bubble* may have been perceived as just another empty entry into a oversaturated genre, but the metaphor for manhandled freedom extends beyond a surface level cinematic context, reflecting a broader cultural backlash against authority present at the time.

Life magazine snapped an iconic image of an auditorium packed with people wearing Anaglyph 3D glasses as they watched Oboler's *Bwana Devil*, in awe of the optical novelty. In an act of subversion, the picture was reused as the cover photo for Guy Debord's *The Society of the Spectacle* (a Separatist book published the year after *The Bubble* was released) as a representation for alienation caused by capitalism. 20 years later, a follow up text was released - the same year that John Carpenter's cult-classic criticism on blind consumption, *They Live* (1988), hit cinemas - a film featuring glasses made to reveal hidden secrets similar to the purpose of 3D glasses. One must wonder what Arch Oboler (who passed in 1987) would have had to say about a modern society whose omnipresent controller no longer requires a physical "bubble" to keep us at bay. Smartphones have since created bubbles around each of us wherever we go, commanding our attention so that we can't even separate from them to be distracted by a movie. That truth may be more frightening than any fiction Oboler envisioned. Zoinks!

THE X FROM OUTER SPACE

1967/1968

BRIAN R. SOLOMON

If Shochiku Corporation's *The X from Outer Space* isn't the most bizarre and unorthodox of all Japanese *kaiju* flicks, then it certainly has to be a very serious contender. In a genre that was dominated by Toho's Godzilla, followed in fame and success by Daiei's Gamera, scanning down the pecking order several rungs will bring us to that loveable D-lister Guilala, the Eric Roberts of giant movie monsters. Part lizard, part chicken, part television antenna, he is a creature that defies proper description, in a movie whose charm and entertainment value is undeniable, despite its relative obscurity.

CINEMA BIZARRO

With the so-called *"kaiju* boom" in full force in Japan by the mid-1960's, the venerable film studio Shochiku, one of the country's oldest and most respected, had decided to jump on the bandwagon and get into the horror and science fiction business. Although best known for prestige dramas and other high-end output, they would get to work cranking out a series of genre pictures which, though supremely odd, would benefit from the studio's hallmark production values and attention to detail. Included in the stream of fascinating stuff that came from Shochiku in the late 1960's were films like *Genocide* (1968), *Goke, Body Snatcher from Hell* (1968, discussed in a later chapter), and *The Living Skeleton* (1968).

But leading the pack would be a movie that in Japan was originally called *Uchi Daikaija Karar* (*Giant Space Monster Guilala*). It came from a concept that was partially concocted by Kazui Nihonmatsu, a second unit director for Shochiku who likely saw the film as an opportunity for him to slip into the main director's chair, which it was. In fact, the studio was so pleased with his work on this one, he was also dispatched to direct *Genocide* the following year, although that film would mark the end of his directorial career, for reasons unknown. It certainly couldn't have been due to the results of his directing work, which are wonderful.

Beautifully lit and shot in Technicolor glory, *The X from Outer Space* will please any *kaiju* fan accustomed to the bright and shiny production values of the best of the Toho science fiction films of the same period, and may, in fact, surpass them in that department. The visuals are pressed into service to tell the tale of a mysterious alien spore that is brought back to Earth by the unwitting crew of a Japanese spacecraft. When the spore is accidentally exposed to acid while the swingin' '60's crew is too busy partying, it mutates into a gigantic creature that could accurately be described as extremely ridiculous — in the most complimentary way, of course.

You can probably figure out the rest. Stomping everything in sight, blasting fireballs, the creature — solemnly given the name "Guilala" by very serious government agents, for whatever reason — goes on a rampage of destruction. A garish blend of seemingly random items found in Shochiku's special effects workshop, the Guilala monster design is almost like a parody of the kinds of *kaiju* that were being presented by Toho in the Godzilla series, or as opponents of Ultraman in the Tsuburaya Productions TV series of the same name. It's unclear if it was meant to be taken as a figure of fun, but what is clear is that viewing it that way makes the movie infinitely more enjoyable — whether your consciousness is enhanced or not during the viewing experience.

Adding to the kitschy shenanigans is a quirky score by composer Taku Izumi, a journeyman whose career would later divert into the highly profitable world of children's anime. Here, he provides music that somehow feels perfectly appropriate to the goings on, blending groovy 1960's pop sounds with even groovier bossa nova influences for the perfect soundtrack to go along with the sight of a 200-story, alien lizard-chicken thing tramping through the Japanese countryside.

The cast is distinguished by the presence of Biloxi, Mississippi's own Peggy Neal, who may very well have been the first example of a minor tradition in Japanese science fiction films of blonde American women in peril. While attending university in Japan, Neal found herself embarking on a short-lived acting career that had included Toei's *Terror Beneath the Sea* the previous year and would eventually include the totally insane *Latitude Zero* for Toho the following year (see *Giant Beast Cinema*). Her acting here is atrocious, but that's not what we come to movies like this for, so that's not a problem. Besides, her efforts to register abject fright are nothing if not impressive in their total commitment.

Of course, the various flustered military and science personnel do eventually win the day when they're able to concoct a foam using a material named — what else — Guilalalium, which, when the beast is coated with it, causes Guilala to shrink back down to his spore form. He can then be contained and shot it into permanent orbit around the sun, no longer a threat to humanity.

All in all, the film is an ambitious attempt by a studio that is stepping outside of its comfort zone to do something wildly different. Unfortunately, the movie (and the monster) never attained the notoriety in Japan that those from more established monster-based studios would enjoy. This carried over into the US where it never got a theatrical release, but was instead brought directly to television by perennial shlock purveyor American International Pictures.

CINEMA BIZARRO

Although he may be just about the most obscure of all Japanese *kaiju*, Guilala did eventually pop up again a couple of times, although much later. Believe it or not, there was something of a "sequel" produced some 40 years later by Shochiku, the *kaiju* parody *Monster X Strikes Back: Attack the G8 Summit*. And in the most improbable of all cameos, Guilala was featured the same year in an American television commercial for a job recruitment website, appearing in classic form trampling a terrified city, while tiny baby Guilalas scamper around in his wake. The rumor at the time was that the advertiser wanted to use Godzilla in the commercial, but was unable to secure the very expensive rights, and so went with a much more affordable alternative. Which is for the best anyway, since the oddness and randomness of it all somehow perfectly suits the legacy of such an offbeat movie and monster.

A hidden gem for those vintage-era *kaiju* and Japanese genre film enthusiasts looking for something a little more off-the-beaten-path from the usual irradiated dinosaurs and giant flying turtles, *The X from Outer Space* is great fun, especially if you can turn your brain off for a solid 90 minutes. Despite the often-unearned reputation of films like this, it is most certainly not a small-budget B-picture, even if it was treated as such on late-night American TV. The quality of the production is evident on the screen, making this film completely worthy of inclusion in the canon of the golden age of Japanese special effects pictures. Most importantly, it isn't afraid of the inherent goofiness of its premise, which is more than can be said of some of the more dour and super-serious productions seen in later years during the wave of Japanese monster movies of the '80's and '90's.

THE GREEN SLIME

1968

DAN MADIGAN

With the success of legendary Italian director Mario Bava's 1965 masterpiece *Planet of the Vampires*, Italy's thirst for outer space storytelling was far from being quenched, so that task fell into the extremely capable hands of prolific filmmaker, Antonio Margheriti. American-based MGM approached Margheriti to create a series of films involving the Gamma-One space station. This quadrilogy of space operas are mostly known by their English titles: *War of the Planets*, *The Wild, Wild Planet*, *The War Between the Planets*, and *The Snow Devils*. 1968's *The Green Slime* is the official, unofficial fifth installment, a cultural fusion of an Italian, retro-futuristic aesthetic with Japanese *kaiju* monsters and good ol' American high testosterone-fueled heroism.

Unlike the previous four films, *The Green Slime* would not be shot in Rome but in Japan at Toei Studios, the creative force behind such diverse classics as the *Johnny Sokko and His Flying Robot* series and the spicy *The Female Convict Scorpion* films. It was created from a story by co-producer Ivan Reiner and written by Tom Rowe, Charles

CINEMA BIZARRO

Sinclair, and Bill Finger (the often uncredited and unheralded co-creator of Batman).

Directed by Kinji Fukasaku, the highly prolific genre filmmaker who created some of the greatest gangster films of any era, *The Green Slime* is an artistic departure from his usual, tightly-terse crime dramas, but the final result is a candy-coated, rubber-suited, monster-filled mêlée. This assignment came to Fukasaku after his previous film, the perversely campy crime drama, *Black Lizard*, became a hit and was a critical success for Shochiku Studios. A career that crossed all genre barriers, Fukasaku is responsible for some of Japan's greatest films and international productions with star-studded casts. He co-directed the World War 2 epic, *Tora! Tora! Tora!* He created the highly influential, nihilistically-themed Yakuza series, *Battles Without Honor and Humanity*, and his swan song was the completion of the widely controversial, ultra-violent masterpiece, *Battle Royale* (2000), from which *The Hunger Games* either "paid homage" or just plain old ripped-off. And along the way, he worked with a who's who of Japan's tough-guy actors: Tetsuya Watari, Bunta Sugawara, real life crime lord Noboru Ando and a long association with the iconic Sonny Chiba and the legendary Toshiro Mifune.

The story starts off in the near future, when the Gamma-3 space station, under the multi-national UNSC (United Nations Space Command), notices that a giant, rogue asteroid is on a collision course to Earth within ten hours, with global annihilation following in its wake (Ten hours? Was anyone paying attention to the radar screens?). To thwart this planet-killing asteroid, named Flora (Flora? Really? Is that the *only* name UNSC scientists could come up with for this massive earth-destroying rock of death that endangers all of humanity?), cue our stoic hero, Commander Jack Rankin (Robert Horton of TV's *Wagon Train* fame) who, channelling his best Doug McClure demeanor and toting Jack Lord's hair, is pulled out of retirement and back into action because apparently, no one else in the service of protecting the world has his specific skills (what they are I still don't know). "Rankin" was an interesting name choice, given Toei was simultaneously creating all the animation for Rankin/Bass' *The King King Show* cartoon for US television.

Rankin is sent to Gamma-3 to take charge of the station, which happens to be under the control of Commander Vince Elliot (solid B-movie regular, Richard Jaeckel), a buzz-cut, tightly-wound gym teacher who's perpetually on the verge of having agita or an aneurysm. In a well-worn plot device, Rankin and Elliot used to be best friends, and to add more fuel to the fire of friction, Elliott's romantic partner is Dr. Lisa Benson, who used to be Rankin's love interest. Benson is played by Italian actress Luciana Paluzzi, who in this film goes between two facial expressions: pouty and poutier. But give Luciana her due; her varied film and television career ranged from AIP films like *Muscle Beach Party* to the Fernando Di Leo poliziotteschi, *The Italian Connection*, but is best known to the world as SPECTRE assassin Fiona Volpe in *Thunderball*. This love triangle, an isosceles of infidelity, fires up the smoldering embers of jealousy between Rankin and Elliot, with Dr. Benson giving enough mixed signals to the ego-driven Rankin that it creates an atmosphere of aggravation for everyone onboard.

Fighting the ticking clock of Fate, our heroes take a space shuttle from Gamma-3 to the surface of Flora, which looks like a massive, floating blood-clot. There, our heroic crew drills into the surface to plant explosives to destroy the potentially earth-shattering asteroid (I'm sure the scribes behind *Armageddon* watched this film with plagiaristic glee). While on Flora, our eponymously monstrous characters, in their embryonic viscid state (resembling glowing globs of viridescent aspic), sneakily latch onto one of the crew and stow away onto the Gamma-3 station. Before you can say, "What the hell was that?", there is a Green Slime infestation running amok throughout the space station.

The titular terrors of *The Green Slime* grow in size and spawn into a fast-breeding species of cyclopean mutants. With their long, flaying, electrically-charged tentacles and miserable, high-pitched, screeching voices, they resemble a legion of histrionically-affected Sigmund and the Sea Monsters covered in interplanetary herpes. Conventional weapons of the day, futuristic laser blasters, are used against the slimy interlopers, but have an adverse effect: when wounded, the creatures' spilled green blood mutates into more slimy interlopers. This cosmic Hydra-like condition makes it impossible to destroy these obnoxious, fast-breeding, little buggers. The gauntlet has been thrown down: how to stop these things before they take over Gamma-3 and then eventually make their way to earth? The decision is made by Rankin to abandon the space-station and detonate it with the Green Slime creatures clinging to the hull... so the Gamma-3 station is blown up... over the earth!

This happens after Rankin ominously tells Dr. Benson that even one drop of Green Slime blood on earth could see these creatures spawn and take over the planet... yet he explodes the Gamma-3 directly over the earth, sending debris and monster body parts hurtling towards an unsuspecting population. Not exactly the most well-thought-out use of the self-destruction method. At least in *Alien*, Ripley blew up the Nostromo deep in outer space and not directly over our home planet.

One thing that is in abundance on Gamma-3, besides the overwrought, mono-eyed monstrosities, is an amazing amount of insubordination directed at Commander Rankin's authority. Elliot defies his rule, Dr. Benson disobeys his commands, and chief medical officer, Dr. Halversen (Ted Gunther) ignores his instructions. Can anyone on Gamma-3 follow goddamn orders?

The Green Slime may not be cinematic gold, but it sure is the pyrite of pulpy schlockiness. Campy and colorful, there is no denying there is a Saturday morning cartoon charm to this movie, one of the many reasons it has always been a favorite of mine. The monsters look like they came more from the hallucinogenic imagination of Sid and Marty Krofft than from Japanese special-effects guru Eiji Tsuburaya's oeuvre. Yukio Manoda and Akira Watanabe, Toho alumni, don't get the credit they deserve for creating outer space ogres that seemingly slithered out of a sugar-induced adolescent nightmare. The film is a hi-fructose phantasm of fun.

For my money, the *piece de resistance* of this film is the psychedelic opening theme song, a kaleidoscopic composition of psychotropic awesomeness conceived by legendary surf music drummer, Richard Delvy, who played with such famous instrumental groups as The Bel-Airs and The Challengers. A tune once heard is not easily forgotten.

GOKÉ
Body Snatcher From Hell

1968/1977

BRIAN R. SOLOMON

If you happen to love this film, then you're in good company. None other than Quentin Tarantino has mentioned it among his favorites, and it's not hard to understand why, given his body of work and movie sensibilities. A strange, visceral, yet also thought-provoking emotional ride, the film is part science fiction, part horror, and part social commentary. Although a rather obscure release from a studio not generally known for such pictures, it has found a very passionate cult following that has only grown over time.

Film studio Shochiku Co. was best known for its thoughtful, even cerebral, "serious" fare, so it stands to reason that when they dipped their feet into the waters of Japan's "*tokusatsu* boom" of special effects movies in the 1960's, the outcome would be different from what audiences were used to. And this movie is perhaps the best demonstration of that, being a magnetic hybrid of a horror survival picture and a highbrow Russian stage drama. The interaction between the characters is the driving force of the film, much more so than the bells and whistles that movies like this typically boast.

Loosely developed from *Gokemidoro*, a popular sci-fi TV series of the time, the story and screenplay were developed by two individuals: sci-fi television veteran Susumu Takaku, whose vast resume would come to include such crossover anime and *tokusatsu* hits as *Cutie Honey* and the *Sentai* series that would later come to the U.S. as *Power Rangers*, and studio stalwart, Kyuzo Kabayashi, who would also pen another Shochiku horror release, *The Living Skeleton*, the same year. Together, they put together the tale of a diverse cast of characters on an airplane who face a double threat: A hijacker among them, and a sinister, vampiric alien presence on the island on which they crash-land.

Downed by both the scheming of the hijacker, played memorably by Hideo Ko, and the interference of a nearby UFO, the passengers must figure out a way to survive as they inevitably turn on one another and the alien entity asserts itself. The hijacker himself is the first to fall and be possessed by the alien vampire, which takes the form of a gelatinous goo that enters the hijacker's body through a vertical gash in his face in the film's most famous scene. From there, the more rational protagonists try to form a strategy, while others only seem to be able to make things worse.

It's a formula which genre fans may also recognize from George Romero's *Night of the Living Dead*, released the same year. Under the direction of Hajime Sato, sci-fi and horror workhorse perhaps best known for *Terror Beneath the Sea* (1966) starring Sonny Chiba, the characters all seem very real, and much more fleshed-out than in typical films of this variety. They also seem to represent different aspects of society. There's the angry young man, the pilot, the scientist, the psychiatrist, the politician, the American, the industrialist and his cuckolding wife, and so on. They're social archetypes, but also feel like real people, with real concerns, real fears, and real motivations. It also helps that the acting is quite accomplished, giving the viewer the impression that extensive ensemble rehearsals were done in preparation for filming.

GOKE, BODY SNATCHER FROM HELL

Among them, Eizo Kitamura shines as the conniving, greedy, and utterly selfish Senator Gozo Mano, who manipulates his way through the film in reprehensible fashion, willing to do anything to survive. American actress Kathy Horan, who also had small parts in Shochiku sci-fi releases *The X from Outer Space* (1967) and *Genocide* (1968), not to mention Toho's *King Kong Escapes* (1967) and *Latitude Zero* (1969) (see chapters on the latter two in our previous book, *Giant Beast Cinema*), pulls off a very sympathetic role as the widow of a Vietnam War soldier, speaking all her lines in subtitled English. Masaya Takahashi is the voice of reason, Dr. Toshiyuki Sagai, who meets a grim end in the film's final moments.

Indeed, it's a grim tale overall, as even the plane's two surviving protagonists, pilot Sugisaka (Teruo Yoshida) and stewardess Kazumi Asakura (Tomomo Sato) are faced in the final scene with the realization that the alien vampire was but the vanguard of an invading force. The movie ends with an entire fleet of alien spaceships approaching Earth in an imminent attack. Many Japanese genre pictures of this period, influenced by World War II and the atomic bomb attacks, take a cynical view of humanity and its chances (or worthiness) for survival; few are as bleak as this one.

The film did not make it to American shores for nine years, when it was finally distributed to television by Pacemaker Films in a hatchet-job of a dub and edit that omits nearly all the film's cast and crew credits and retitles it simply *Body Snatcher from Hell* (the original Japanese release had been called *Kyūketsuki Gokemidoro*, literally translated as *Vampire Gokemidoro*.) It did not get a true, proper release in its original form in the United States until 2012, when it was put out by the Criterion Collection as part of its Eclipse series in a DVD box set called, *When Horror Came to Shochiku*.

Nevertheless, the film made an impression on many American television viewers in the 1970's and 1980's, Tarantino among them. In fact, it's been pointed out that the opening scene of *Goke, Body Snatcher from Hell*, which features a miniature of an airplane flying through a vividly red-tinted skyscape, is very similar to a scene in Tarantino's *Kill Bill Vol. 1* (2003) in which Uma Thurman's Bride flies to Japan to meet with the legendary sword maker Hattori Hanzo (who happens to be played by Hajime Sato's former collaborator, Sonny Chiba). It remained an artifact of late-night television in the English-speaking world until very recent times, with its profile rising significantly over the past dozen or so years amongst those who seek out cinema that's just a little bit different.

In addition to Tarantino, the influence of *Goke, Body Snatcher from Hell* can be seen in the later work of many horror filmmakers, including Romero, John Carpenter, David Cronenberg, and others. Like all great movies of its kind, it germinated in the minds of individuals who would later go on to become great creators in their own right. And for those who think they know all there is to know about Japanese *tokusatsu* cinema, or who seek to dismiss and defame it, this is the perfect film to use as a counterpoint to demonstrate what a fertile, creatively varied, and surprisingly intellectual time this was for Japanese sci-fi films. Honestly, the Americans were still catching up during this period, and it wouldn't be until the 1970's that they'd be producing anything on the level of what was being done in Japan.

Goke, the Body Snatcher from Hell is a surprisingly thoughtful meditation on class, society, gender relations, generational conflict, and more. But aside from all that thought-provoking stuff, make no mistake—it delivers the goods. If you just want to see a flick in which aliens that look like spilled shampoo ooze their way into people's faces and turn them into blood-sucking killers, then this movie has you covered. Either way, you'll have a good time.

Weird West Roundup

Of the 1930s

LARRY BLAMIRE

If a 1930's western title contains the words "ghost," "phantom" or "terror," there's a fair chance it will contain *none* of these things. I have spent years seeking out westerns with cross-genre elements, stubbornly sticking to the term "Horror Western". Given that it excluded, among other things, science fiction, I finally caved to the broader appellation "Weird Western". Now, I personally consider "old dark house movies" horror, despite their lack of supernatural elements, provided they're drenched in atmosphere. My criteria is similar with westerns; a bit of mystery, a dash of strangeness and foreboding, a trace of sci-fi, and I'm satisfied. Cowboy star Ken Maynard enjoyed success with several spooky silents, but it wasn't until the first sound decade that they seemed to flourish. If you're unfamiliar with such low budget 54-minute wonders, be prepared to hear the words "deed", "ranch", "mine", and "treasure" ad infinitum, as you marvel at the number of bad guys willing to "Scooby Doo" the heck out of poor innocents.

Though the 1930 release *Under Texas Skies* featured a gorilla-like brute with a proclivity for walking up to the lens, horror-movie-style, it wasn't until mid-1932 that we saw a wave of western weirdness, a brushfire I like to think was sparked by that earlier film's success. These five 1932 films seem to lay down templates for things to come.

RKO's *Ghost Valley*, headlining cowboy star, Tom Keene (*Plan 9 from Outer Space*), opens promisingly with a lantern moving through the nighttime streets of an actual ghost town (Hornitos: a production value bonanza) as wind howls. Even by day, the location is stark and gritty, providing sharp-eyed cinematographer Ted McCord with a moody canvas. As often happens, a young lady (Merna Kennedy) arrives to claim her inheritance, in this case, the mine. Shadowy clutching hands, secret passageways, spooky organ music, and a mysterious phantom are, for reasons known only to director Fred Allen and screenwriter Adele Buffington, completely undercut early on by showing the bad guys discussing their manufactured ghostly shenanigans, an annoying and inexplicable move all too prevalent in these kinds of films. Nonetheless, thanks largely to McCord's camera, it still entertains, even when hero Keene tests the practicality of riding a horse while holding a cape across his lower face when he impersonates the phantom. There is also some impressive and harrowing staging on an actual suspended ore cart.

Fox's *Mystery Ranch* has more teeth, with its moody, gothic opening of a rider strangled in a storm, horror-lit closeups of the great Charles Middleton (*Strangler of the Swamp*, Ming in *Flash Gordon*) playing grim piano as he smiles at the silhouette of a hanging man, and a large, silent, homicidal henchman (Noble Johnson, a year before *King Kong*). It promises a more serious approach and largely delivers via its madman-ruling-valley trope. Hero George O'Brien is more natural than many contemporaries, aided by David Howard's capable direction, smooth camerawork from Joseph H. August and George Schneiderman, an early Hugo Friedhofer score, and an angelic Cecilia Parker. Though the horror vibe lessens, the largely sinister mood prevails.

Monogram's *Hidden Valley*, from prolific writer-director Robert N. Bradbury, is more notable for the door it opens than the goods it delivers. Bradbury casts his son, cowboy star Bob Steele, as guide to an archaeologist searching for a vanished lost tribe, with the promise of treasure. The adventurous spell of the majestic scenery is broken when Bob is accused of murder, bogging us down in courtroom and standard western fare before returning to the wilderness. One should note here the commingling of horses and horseless carriages that proliferated in B-Westerns, setting them in their own strange cross-time. Even odder, the climax makes vigorous use of the Goodyear Blimp; a wonderfully incongruous sight over the desert. But, better "lost civilization" westerns were just around the bend. The movie's talk of conquistadors and El Diablo Mountain reminds us that Bob Steele played the irritable sheriff in 1958's *Giant from the Unknown* (which I wrote about in the previous volume, *Giant Beast Cinema*).

Warners entered the fray next with *Haunted Gold*, featuring a young John Wayne in early Poverty Row phase, produced by future Looney Tunes boss, Leon Schlesinger (here, recycling his 1928 Ken Maynard silent *The Phantom City*). This one jumps out and says "boo" right away, from animated bats and spooky main titles, to Leon Forbstein's Universal-like music, to the great Nicholas Musuraca's high-angle camera of nervous outlaws (including perennial bad guy, Harry Woods) huddled around a table. Turns out they, John Wayne, and everyone else have been invited by persons unknown. This use of the "invisible host" setup in film actually predates both *The Ninth Guest* (1934) and Agatha Christie's novel *And Then There Were None*, published in 1939. Wayne also receives a warning from "The Phantom" to stay away from the "haunted mine". It's unfortunate that such an atmospheric setup (eyes watching behind pictures, howling wolves, shadowy clutching hands, hooded phantom) trails off somewhat. Even more regrettable is that Wayne's sidekick, played by actor and former Negro Leagues ball player Edgar Hughes "Blue" Washington, is the constant subject of some of the most egregious racism, helping to sour an otherwise entertaining entry.

"Stranger, don't let the sun go down on you here," reads a crude sign, followed by the incongruous imagery (Ted McCord's camera again) of a distant, black-cloaked figure skittering across starkly bleached rocks that seem harsh and primitive.

Tombstone Canyon, our final release of 1932, written by Claude Rister, directed by Alan James, offers no gun-toting ghosts, no damsels with deeds, but the first of the sagebrush serial killers. The lack of a music score, with long silences broken by the Phantom Killer's chuckle or chilling cry, lend a dreamlike quality that embraces the film's limited budget. And when his shriek is heard, someone dies. This is not a whodunit, so it's no spoiler to say that the killer is played by silent screen actor Sheldon Lewis, who looks particularly alarming in a candlelit cabin scene, as makeup, cloak, and wide slouch hat seem to evoke both Conrad Veidt's *The Man Who Laughs* and the Joker that Veidt later inspired. The relentlessly grim mood makes this one a favorite.

Ken Maynard is back in 1934 with some very different weirdness, desperately slapping together the notorious *Smoking Guns* to cover some exotic vacations he charged to Universal. This takes a wrongly-accused Maynard to South America for some vicious crocodile action, then back to the States seeking answers in a spooky old house. The results are bizarre and unintentionally hilarious, feeling made-up-as-you-go (Ken addresses people as "man" several times, sounding oddly contemporary). Best of all, he takes the place of a guy he doesn't look like — and *nobody notices*. It was his last film for the studio, but no one can say it isn't entertaining.

John Wayne returns as *The Star Packer* (no, not the prized employee at a meat-processing facility), notable for a mystery villain (the Shadow) who gives orders through a fake wall safe (shades of Edgar Wallace), plus some shots "fired from nowhere." It seems to matter little to writer-director Robert Bradbury that the villain's identity is obvious.

More outré is *The Rawhide Terror*, written and directed by Jack Nelson, intended as a serial until cash problems brutally cut it to forty-seven minutes. A film that possibly I alone love, it is important not to think about this one too much, and by "too much" I mean, at all. At some point the hero gives way to a supporting player who then becomes the hero (!), with nary an explanation. But I enjoy the unintended surrealism of its disjointed narrative and its creepy vibe, especially the outrageous title character (another bizarre serial killer), whose tracks vanish up Ghost Mountain, who strangles at will (among other methods), dresses off-the-wall and is so goofily what-just-happened-to-my-brain in close-ups that he needs to be seen. As with *Tombstone Canyon*, there is no music score, to its betterment.

1935 brought what is likely the world's most beloved science fiction western musical, the serial *The Phantom Empire*, starring Gene Autry; a Weird Western landmark. Here, the promise of Hidden Valley explodes with lost underground civilizations, advanced technology and that beloved sci-fi fixture: the boxy robot. "The scientific city of Murania," as it's called, just happens to be under Autry's Radio Ranch where he broadcasts his shows. It's also a source of "a fortune in radium", which bad guys want. In Murania, the descendants of Mu, under Queen Tika (Dorothy Christy), seek to quash a rebellion, even as legends of their helmeted "Thunder Riders" inspire a tin-hatted fan club, led by young Frankie Darro. The entrance to Murania turns out to be Bronson Caves, outfitted with a kind of garage door worked by a robot. Otto Brewer and Breezy Eason direct the fun, which looks downright lavish for tight-fisted Nat Levine's Mascot Pictures. Models and process shots are surprisingly good, making this the best blend of sagebrush, songs, and sci-fi ever.

From the moment mining engineer Larry Sutton (Randolph Scott) rides into a small mountain community and finds a corpse in a cabin, we know we're in different territory with Paramount's *The Rocky Mountain Mystery* (also known as *The Fighting Westerner*), adapted by Ethel Doherty from Zane Grey's unpublished *Golden Dreams*. Directed by Charles Barton, with a cast including Ann Sheridan and Kathleen Burke (Lota, the panther woman in the 1932 *Island of Lost Souls*), this one casts a spell of dread from the get-go, due in no small part to its vivid location (beneath the shadow of a foreboding and rundown stamp mill) and an inspired use of sound. Creaking boards shift like restless bones in the walls, in chorus with howling winds, lorded over by the ominous pounding of the stamp mill; a hellish variation on the Morlock's underground machines in George Pal's *The Time Machine*. Notably gruesome murders, engineered by a figure in black, cause fear to hang over the gathered relatives, giving it a Western, old dark house feel. Even the comic relief of Chic Sale's acting sheriff (the closest thing to Scott's sidekick) is appropriately muted, making this one of the most satisfying of dark 1930's Westerns and a personal favorite.

The remainder of 1935 consisted of another Robert Bradbury/Bob Steele collaboration *Big Calibre*, notable for its use of poison gas capsules as murder weapons and a crazy chemist villain whose disguise is almost as whacked as *The Rawhide Terror*. Once again, Bradbury does not seem to care that it's easy to guess whodunit.

CINEMA BIZARRO

In *Vanishing Riders*, Bill Cody and a kid dress up as skeletons to terrorize outlaws. The best scene has bad guy leader Wally Wales storming into his outlaw camp, berating his gang for loudly singing about how they are outlaws.

1936's *Desert Phantom*, an improvement on a 1932 Harry Carey film, *The Night Rider*, gives us yet another mystery killer, with a touch of locked-room mystery, investigated by an amiable Johnny Mack Brown.

Ghost Patrol with Tim McCoy is a western take on that favorite 30's trope: the ray that can knock planes out of the sky. One refreshing note is that McCoy's sidekick, Henry (James P. Burtis), is a no-nonsense model of efficiency; a refreshing change from the usual bumbler.

But it's 1937's *Riders of the Whistling Skull* that brings the significant 1930's Weird Westerns to a close. Once again, we have legends of a lost city, this time sparking a sizable expedition with none other than Republic's revolving trio of cowboy heroes, the Three Mesquiteers, represented by their A-team: Bob Livingston, Ray "Crash" Corrigan and Max Terhune (the one who rode the range with ventriloquist dummy Elmer). When an expedition member is murdered, they quickly realize there's a killer in their midst. This is pure pulp mystery, action, and adventure, epitomized by its striking visual of an enormous demonic-looking rock skull, successfully delivering the Saturday Matinee goods on a modest budget.

Then, as Universal horror subsided somewhat, post-mid-30s, so it seemed, did the Weird Western… *or did it?*

Weird West Roundup
★
Of the 1940s

LARRY BLAMIRE

Though 1930's Weird Westerns seemed to parallel that decade's horror boom, there is no apparent similar pattern for the 1940's. And while this decade might have had less sinister six-guns in number, it more than makes up for it with some genuine gold-strikes later on.

In order of release, we first have 1941's moderately entertaining *The Lone Rider in Ghost Town*. "Nobody goes near Parker's Diggings," reads the ominous warning at the mine. A man's gone missing in one of the abandoned shafts and George Houston and scrappy sidekick Al "Fuzzy" St. John investigate. They make a pretty good team, and, though Houston might seem an odd fit for a cowboy star, given his operatic background, he makes a vigorous and robust hero. There's a fair amount of action (at one point, two groups on horseback pull guns and start shooting, like it's the thing to do), and it's well shot by Jack Greenhalgh, with the prerequisite creeping around spooky tunnels, trap doors, and a pretty convincing ghost town.

That same year, sagebrush strangeness went south of the border with *La Vuelta del Charro Negro* (*Return of the Black Rider*), featuring a fancy-dressed cowboy hero investigating the desecration of graves, leading to a mad scientist working with mummy parts in the catacombs. To date, no English subtitled print exists, but it's fairly easy to follow. An overabundance of screen time is given to a comic relief duo who have some kind of water finder, and horror elements come a bit late and are fairly mild. The film is almost entirely scored with Rimsky-Korsakov's *Scheherazade*, until the spooky parts give way to Bach's familiar *Toccata and Fugue in D Minor*. The hero could throw better punches, and he always seems to be escaping (there's a five-minute stretch where no less than three people get knocked out), but the film is an interesting look at what may be Mexico's first Weird Western. And how many movies can boast songs and grave-robbing?

Released a month later in 1941 was *The Shepherd of the Hills*, an unusual film worthy of greater attention. It might be more of an Eastern than a Western, but John Wayne's presence (beginning his A-list period), the movie's loving embrace of the great outdoors and its overall look, certainly make it close kin. More importantly, it embodies the overlap of Weird Western and folk horror in its depiction of a forbidden place (the enticingly named Moanin' Meadow) steeped in superstition. "That's where the ha'nt comes from... frogs as quiet as grave rocks and light comin' from nowhere. Trees don't rustle and flowers grow big, but they don't have pretty smells." Its exploration of the roots of this cursed land (stained family history and years of dysfunction and resentment) that could harvest such a manifestation, results in something poetic and haunting. "Them that goes in there has daylight dreams." Directed with loving detail by Henry Hathaway, from a novel by Harold Bell Wright, the movie exudes intoxicating atmosphere and its characters are breathed into rich reality by Wayne, Harry Carey Sr., Beulah Bondi, Marc Lawrence, Marjorie Main, James Barton, and especially Betty Field, whose performance I find incredibly affecting.

WEIRD WEST ROUNDUP OF THE 1940s

1941 comes to a close with *Saddle Mountain Roundup*, and I am telling you right now that as far as I know, there is no saddle, no mountain, and no roundup. There is, however, the first 40's Weird Western with satisfying horror vibes. This is another in the Range Busters series, with Ray "Crash" Corrigan, John "Dusty" King, and Max "Alibi" Terhune, which means of course Alibi's ventriloquist dummy Elmer, and that's some grade-A weirdness right there, like when the two of them are conversing alone on the trail, or when Elmer's on a bad guy's lap and starts talking to him (huh?). The film opens on a dark and stormy night at Harper Ranch with crabby, paranoid, old Magpie Harper (John Elliott), his pet raven on the back of his chair, some quietly sinister music, and a skulking figure in a black rain slicker. There's more shot coverage than most small budgets allow, and director S. Roy Luby takes advantage (closeup of Harper, whip-pan to a hand pressed against window, push in on window, figure whips away into night, cut to closeup of raven). It also sustains its grave atmosphere, offsetting the lightheartedness of so many Weird Westerns at the time. There's a reading of the will, a mysterious trail of match scratches, an underground tunnel, corpses turning up, and a climax cleverly engineered to hide the culprit until the very last second.

1942's *Ghost Town Law* is a Rough Riders movie (yep, another trio) that starts like a standard western but soon has the heroes protecting the heroine in an old dark house connected to a mine via some old tunnels. There's sinister, gothic imagery in a nice low-angle shot of the house with a dark figure clambering around, and at one point, there are queasy, undulating cobwebs that had me rewind.

The Haunted Ranch (1943) is another Range Busters film from Monogram, but it's not quite up to their previous Weird Western, *Saddle Mountain Roundup*. Like many before, it tips its hand too early; the dead giveaway being heavy Glenn Strange (prior to essaying the Frankenstein Monster three times in a row) telling his cronies, "Chuck, you keep up the ghost noises" and "Better get them ghost noises started." An organ that seems to play itself is actually Charles King playing an accordion in a secret room (it's also funny to see the veteran heavy slapping chains around). And when the bad guys question Elmer the dummy we know we're in Odd Town.

That same year brought *Prairie Chickens*, an amusing Hal Roach comedy featuring a bevy (isn't it always?) of beautiful gals at a haunted ranch house (with some outrageous spook costumes), aided by Noah Beery Jr., Jimmy Rogers, and Jack Norton.

Former Flash Gordon and Tarzan, Buster Crabbe starred as Billy Carson, "King of the Wild West" in a series of films for PRC, and *Wild Horse Phantom* (1944) concerns a spooky mine with stolen loot and a cackling "ghost." I normally enjoy Al "Fuzzy" St. John (here, as Fuzzy Q. Jones), but for some reason, he is way more over-the-top than usual. However, the best scene has him and bad guy John Cason hearing screeches in the mine, leading to Fuzzy's extended battle with none other than… the giant bat from the Bela Lugosi film, *The Devil Bat* (1940), making this an odd entry indeed.

Fuzzy is back in form in a later Billy Carson movie, 1946's *Ghost of Hidden Valley*, in which they help an Englishman who inherited the Hidden Valley Ranch (not the dressing). It's a little light on creepy. We should note, however, that Crabbe proves himself a better actor than most cowboy heroes.

It's towards the end of the decade that we come upon a pair of gems; two Hopalong Cassidy movies (both produced by star William Boyd): *The Unexpected Guest* (1947) and *The Dead Don't Dream* (1948). While they may not sound like western titles, I think that's part of the appeal, as these are among the eeriest of oaters. Both directed by George Archainbaud for United Artists, they're a cut above in every department. *The Unexpected Guest* finds Hopalong, Lucky Jenkins (Rand Brooks), and California Carlson (Andy Clyde) riding to California's cousin's house for a reading of the will. In the very opening, we have echoes of 1932's *Tombstone Canyon* as a phantom in black stalks across pale rocks, taking shots at California. The walled-in adobe style ranch seems lonely and desolate, and the presence of jittery Matilda (who talks to spirits), played by none other than Una O'Connor (*The Bride of Frankenstein*), reinforces the horror atmosphere. The ranch has an air of mystery, with a small graveyard where Hoppy sees lurking figures and Matilda receives cryptic messages from an eerie voice: "Go to Hidden Canyon come morning, see three pillars of stone, follow trail up to the top of the hill…" After a candlelit reading of the will, Hoppy declares it motive enough for the six heirs to kill each other off. As he says that, wind blows the candles out and there's a bang. When they're relit, we see one of the relatives dead in his chair. There's also a buffalo head twist on the painted-portrait-with-eyes-that-move gag, and scenes in a basement lit to look like early 30's Universal. Director Archainbaud maintains suspense right up until its breathless reveal.

The Dead Don't Dream is less drenched in atmosphere at first, but gains unsettling traction as it goes. This finds our three heroes heading for the exact same ranch set, but here, it's a troubled and gloomy inn where Lucky is to meet up with his fiancé Mary for their wedding. Things are derailed when Mary's uncle goes missing; the latest in a series of disappearances at the inn. *The Dead Don't Dream* becomes sort of a western take on the oft-filmed *The Secret of the Blue Room*, where a room is thought cursed. This one benefits from a high body count and no shortage of suspects. There's also a mine (mines sure were popular) where we get a nifty visual of the phantom killer poised below an enormous hanging rock. Throughout both films, Boyd plays Hoppy as something of a range detective; alternately cheery, brash, no-nonsense, and dryly amusing. And not only is the building location the same, but our heroes even stay in the same room set, complete with door to the balcony (used by Hoppy for surveillance in both films). Boyd gets to utter that immortal line, "The killer is right in this room." Again, Archainbaud keeps things tight and fast-moving. Both films benefit from intelligent scripts (Ande Lamb and Francis Rosenwald, respectively) and eerie, evocative scores (David Chudnow and Darrell Calker, respectively).

I had *Rimfire* (1949) on the low end of a DVD Double feature (I got it for *Little Big Horn*) for years before finally giving it a spin. What a pleasant surprise, as *Rimfire* teeters on horror for most of its runtime. A professional gambler, the Abilene Kid (*Racket Squad*'s Reed Hadley), is falsely accused of cheating and railroaded to a hanging, but not before cursing everyone responsible. And by golly, if they don't start dying. A lot. Each one is found with a different card, beginning with the deuce of spades. In the very first killing, we hear what is clearly Reed Hadley's voice from a window in the dark of night… "Lamson… go for your gun," followed by a shot from the darkness. And so it goes, with a body count into double digits.

Fear grips the town as headlines scream "Ghost Killer on Rampage." Each victim is offed by a gold, rimfire bullet. It's briskly directed by Reeves "Breezy" Eason (his last such effort), with writing credited to Arthur St. Clair, Frank Wisbar, and Ron Ormond, and if the middle name rings a bell, that's because Wisbar wrote and directed PRC's memorable *Strangler of the Swamp* (1946), itself a remake of his 1936 German film, *Fährmann Maria*. In fact, *Rimfire* is essentially another reworking. The frightened town is well-peopled by familiar faces: Henry Hull, George Cleveland, Jason Robards Sr., Mary Beth Hughes, Fuzzy Knight, Chris-Pin Martin, John Cason, and Don C. Harvey, and boy, is it fun to watch them all get jumpy and paranoid. Character actor James Millican, in a rare lead, is the lawman trying to crack the mystery. A delicious bowl of dread hangs over this one, giving us a Weird Western trifecta to end the decade.

In 1950, Columbia released *Streets of Ghost Town*, a Durango Kid film starring Charles Starrett, and I'm letting this one in just under the wire, because, though it's largely stock footage in flashbacks, these are relayed around a table with a single lantern in a rundown saloon, in a ghost town in the middle of the night, which feels like where we came in.

Dinosaurs & Cowboys

THE BEAST OF Hollow Mountain
1956

THE VALLEY OF GWANGI
1969

DAN MADIGAN

It is often the case in Hollywood that more than one film comes from the same source material. In fact, that should be the norm, not the exception. The next two films open for discussion both sprouted from the same fertile seeds of imagination. The sower of those seeds was none other than highly acclaimed special effects genius, Willis O'Brien. You may have heard of him. He was the creative force behind a little film called *King Kong*.

O'Brien's stop-motion wizardry didn't just end on screen. His dexterous fingers were often busy on the typewriter, banging out stories, and one of those was "Valley of the Mist". Although O'Brien was revered in the business, he could not garner traction to see his story come to fruition. So, it languished for several years, gathering dust. The "Valley of the Mist" is a weird hybrid, a combination of two popular genres at the time: Westerns and Dinosaur films. (But the concept of cowboys mixing it up with "monsters" was already filmed and staged magnificently with 1949's *Mighty Joe Young* with Willis O'Brien himself supervising the special effects team, which included a neophyte named Ray Harryhausen. It would win the first Academy Award in the newly created "Special Visual Effects" category.)

The first team to take the creative crack at O'Brien's story would be led by Edward Nassour, a producer of stop-motion animation who, along with his brother William, had been in the special effects business for a while. Edward had worked on a previous dinosaur picture, 1951's *The Lost Continent*, as a special effects supervisor (Edited sequences from that movie ended up in the Americanized, second Godzilla film known in the states as *Gigantis, the Fire Monster*). Nassour knew a thing or two about dinosaurs and that knowledge would lead to his sole directorial effort, *The Beast of Hollow Mountain*.

Sharing his directing duties with Ismail Rodríguez, Nassour also oversaw the special effects personally with Jack Rabin and Louis De-Witt lending their talents to the team. Rodríguez was a popular director of the time and knew how to work with actors, so it appears that he was behind the non-dinosaur scenes. The experienced screenwriting team of Jack DeWitt (Louis' brother) and Robert Hill fleshed out O'Brien's story. Composer Raúl Lavista and cinematographer Jorge Stahl, Jr, both highly prolific and winners of lifetime achievement awards in Mexican cinema, rounded out the core creative force.

The story finds rancher Jimmy Ryan (Guy Madison) and his trusted companion, Felipe Sanchez (Carlos Rivas) perplexed as to why some of their cattle have gone missing. Ryan wrongly believes his business and romantic rival Enrique Rios (Eduardo Noriega) is responsible, but the real culprit behind the cattle disappearance is the titular *Beast of Hollow Mountain*, a prehistoric dinosaur that is a cross between an anemic-looking Allosaurus and a sickly-looking T-Rex.

The film is a lowercase b-movie. Set in Mexico, the story has its perquisite western motifs: fistfights, stampedes, horse-play, an extremely annoying Mexican kid, and a love triangle with sultry Patricia Medina thrown in the mix, but it meanders instead of moving along, and the worst part is, there's no dinosaur action until the last fifteen minutes.

Luckily, by the time this film starts wearing out its welcome, the dreaded Beast appears from the swamps at the foot of Hollow Mountain to cause havoc. Why now? How did this prehistoric creature survive for millions of years? Where are its relatives? How come no one has ever seen one until now? Why the hell am I asking pertinent questions for a story that falls apart under scrutiny? That's just it; *The Beast of Hollow Mountain* is not a film to be held under a critical microscope. This American/Mexican co-production is an adequate time-filler that never goes too far into the western genre nor deep enough into a true horror movie. It's not trying to insult your intelligence by leaving all those above questions unanswered, but then again, it's not challenging your mental dexterity either. The Beast looks more like a concoction of *Gumby* creator, Art Clokey, than today's CGI-infused *Jurassic Park* reptilia; more remedial than original. But the film was made in earnest. Though uneven, you have to admire any film that pits cowboys and dinosaurs against each other. I'm not trying to give *The Beast of Hollow Mountain* a short shrift but if there is one movie you want to see that has cowboys and dinosaurs sharing the screen, then it's the one they made thirteen years later from the same Willis O'Brien story idea, seven years after O'Brien's sudden death.

The Valley of Gwangi is the ultimate cowboy/dinosaur mashup. Directed with a yeoman's efficiency by Jim O'Connolly (*Tower of Evil*), whose career in British cinema has seen him in almost every position behind the camera, from director to production manager, screenwriter to producer, O'Connolly was more than able to helm a heavily effects-laden production. And working alongside American producer Charles H. Schneer, whose successes in fantasy cinema is a rollcall of legendary films, the Warner Bros.-Seven Arts, Inc. production was in capable and experienced hands.

Even though the original concept for *The Valley of Gwangi* came from O'Brien's imagination, it was in turn greatly influenced by Arthur Conan Doyle's *The Lost World*, as well as the 1925 film version of the book, on which O'Brien created the landmark special effects. Screenwriter William Bast, Mystery Writers of America Edgar Award winner, is the scribe of record on *Gwangi*. (BTW "Gwangi" is the word used by many Native American tribes for lizard)

The rousing suite was composed by Oscar nominee, Jerome Moross, and it sounds like a euphonious combination of a Bernard Herrmann composition and Aaron Copland arrangement, which only makes sense because they were both lifelong friends of his.

CINEMA BIZARRO

The story takes place, once again in Mexico, at the turn of the last century. T.J. Breckenridge (played by Israeli beauty Gila Golan but dubbed by an uncredited voice actor) owns and operates a struggling rodeo. Her former flame, Tuck Kirby (James Franciscus, who would go on to star in cult films *Beneath the Planet of the Apes* and *The Cat o' Nine Tails*), who has been working for the Buffalo Bill's Wild West show, re-emerges to persuade T.J. to sell him her under-performing operation. She won't sell, more out of pride than practicality. Stubborn as she is sultry, T.J. believes her potential ace-in-the-hole is a prehistoric, tiny horse she calls El Diablo, which came into her possession through a circuitous route of poaching and theft.

El Diablo, which in reality is an Eohippus, a long-thought-extinct horse, was stolen from the Forbidden Valley. Considered sacred by the local gypsy populous (Mexican Gypsies?), it's a dry, rocky terrain that takes the place of the foreboding Carpathian Mountains for the superstitious gypsies. The movie was partly filmed in Almería, Spain, the barren backdrop for countless, classic spaghetti westerns, and this adds a sense of arid authenticity to the story. Our indigenous troupe, led by the one-eyed Tia Zorina (Freda Jackson) and her malignant dwarf henchman, want to return El Diablo to its rightful home in the valley. Fearing that a curse will fall upon the land if the minuscule mare is not returned, she intends on bringing back that elusive equine at all costs.

Throw into the mix English paleontologist Horace Bromley (Laurence Naismith, who played Argus the ship builder in *Jason and the Argonauts*), who just happens to be foraging in the desert for dinosaur remains, and genre regular Richard Carlson (*Creature from the Black Lagoon*). Both are added to the group of interlopers who dare enter the valley. Everything is a confluence of circumstances to get our characters into the aforementioned Forbidden Valley, which has been untouched by evolution since the Cretaceous Period (that's about 140 million years, give or take a few millennia). The Valley is impregnable, except for a small crevice in the rocky walls that allows Tuck, T.J., and company entry into this "world from another time". Once they enter this taboo tableau, they encounter various prehistoric creatures: a flying Pteranodon, a skittish Ornithomimus, and the boss daddy of the Valley, Gwangi himself, a badass Tyrannosaurus Rex.

This is where *The Valley of Gwangi* becomes a reptilian retelling of *King Kong*, where the motivation becomes exploitation. Both Gwangi and Kong are victims of man's selfish impulses. In Gwangi's case, the attempt to bring back the tiny El Diablo to his sacred place of origin leads to the discovery of the Gwangi by the circus folks and, true to their nature, they see big $$$ in capturing and profiteering off the big green guy's proscenium arch imprisonment.

Two standout sequences are when a band of rodeo riders attempt to rope and capture Gwangi and Gwangi's face-to-face showdown with an impressive looking Styracosaurus. It is not Man's ingenuity that finally subdues Gwangi, but a fortuitous landslide that renders the ferocious lizard unconscious. Gwangi is then imprisoned, hauled off, and is going to be put on display in the middle of the rodeo in Mexico City. I mean, what could go wrong, having a massively, murderously enraged, ravenously unstoppable apex predator smack dab center of a densely populated area with thousands of potential sombrero-wearing snacks milling about? Of course this doesn't bode well, because like Kong, the King Lizard breaks free and chaos reigns as he rampages through the city.

The true star of this movie is a man whose name is synonymous with cinematic visual virtuosity: Ray Harryhausen. A protege of O'Brien when he was a teen, to call Harryhausen a master of special effects is to limit the scope of his greatness. He's the Michelangelo of stop-motion; that is *not* hyperbole.

In O'Brien's original story, Gwangi is an Allosaurus, but when the monstrous lizard comes to life, Gwangi is actually a combination of Allosaurus and Tyrannosaurus Rex. This is the same crossbreeding seen in *The Beast of Hollow Mountain*, but one only has to glance at Harryhausen's creations to see that his technical mastery is far superior to anyone else doing the same work in Hollywood at the time. Harryhausen's visual references were partly based on paleo-artist Charles R. Knight's (1874-1953) brilliant paintings of dinosaurs.

The always resourceful Harryhausen reuses some of his previous ideas that worked well in his earlier pictures. When Gwangi wrestles with the circus elephant, that skirmish is similar to when the Ymir in *20 Million Miles to Earth* has a Texas Death Match with a pachyderm counterpart. Gwangi's fiery, undeserved, demise in a flaming cathedral

CINEMA BIZARRO

echoes the conflagration that consumes the radioactively poisoned Rhedosaurus, who's trapped in a Coney Island rollercoaster in the climax to *The Beast from 20,000 Fathoms*. His menagerie of monsters, mythically inspired or historically accurate, is as eclectic as it is iconic, and I'd be hard pressed to pick any one favorite. It's his entire output that impresses, an oeuvre of amazement nonpareil.

Some critics have said that *The Valley of Gwangi* is a second-tier Harryhausen, but second-tier Harryhausen is better than first-tier anyone else. His skill and craftsmanship are on a level of unparalleled mastery for the time or, frankly, anytime. And timing is everything. If *The Valley of Gwangi* was released in the fifties, it could have been part of the big monster craze. If it came just a few years later, it would have found its niche in the drive-in circuit. But being released when it was, the film found itself floundering in the shifting of cinematic tastes and didn't perform well at the 1969 box-office. Harryhausen himself said that when the film was finishing in post-production, there was a power shift in the studio. Management had no faith in the film, so they spent almost nothing in publicizing it or pushing any promotional effort on a large scale.

It's really not fair to compare these two films side by side, especially when budgetary constraints and technical artistry come into play. The barometer should be this: do these films entertain you? That's their job, to bring enjoyment to the viewer. *Hollow Mountain* may be considered campy and cheesy and *Gwangi* may be lauded as a masterpiece in stop motion animation, but there is no denying that both, in their own prehistoric throwback way, capture that gutsy feeling of the weird western adventure pulps.

CURSE OF THE UNDEAD

1959

PHOEF SUTTON

It's often a fool's errand to start naming the "first" of anything. The first rock and roll song. The first Film Noir. The first science fiction novel. If you pick any one thing, someone will prove you wrong by naming an earlier thing. But I'll go out on a limb and say that *Curse of the Undead* (1959) is the first Vampire Western.

Go ahead and prove me wrong.

I was going to call *Curse of the Undead* the first Horror Western (which many people do), but then I remembered all the "ghost town" Westerns of the 1930's and 1940's: *Haunted Gold* (1932), *Ghost Town Gold* (1936), *Ghost of Hidden Valley* (1946), *Ghost Town Renegades* (1947), and many more, detailed in the two Weird Western Roundup chapters in this book.

This film was written by husband and wife team of Edward and Mildred Dein. In keeping with the self-deprecating humor that typified screenwriters of the era, the Deins said they wrote it as a joke, never

CINEMA BIZARRO

thinking it would get made. I have my doubts. I'm a screenwriter, and I know it takes weeks (at least) of hard to work to write a film script. You don't do that as a joke. In the back of your mind, at least, you hope it will sell.

And sell it they did. To producer Joseph Gershenson. Gershenson is mostly known for being the head of the music department at Universal Pictures during the 50's and 60's, but he also produced a bunch of low-budget movies for Universal in the 40's and 50's: *House of Dracula* (1945), *Monster on Campus* (1958), *The Leech Woman* (1960), and others.

The Deins gave him a good script. It blends the Western tropes with the vampire tropes pretty well. What's more, they actually play with vampire lore in very interesting ways, tracing it back to the actual myths rather than the film clichés. Unfortunately, their script is a bit let down by the unimaginative and rather flat work of the director. This may seem odd, since the director is none other than Edward Dein, one of the co-writers of the script, but the Good Lord doesn't give talent with both hands, and being a pretty good writer doesn't make you a good director.

The film begins in a typical Western town – in the Universal backlot – with a coach being driven down the street by Dr. Carter (John Hoyt) while his daughter Dolores rides next to him, noting all the black wreaths on all the doors. They go into a house where a young girl is dying. Dr. Carter confides to hunky minister Preacher Dan Young (Eric Fleming, just about to start his seven-year run as Gil Favor on *Rawhide*) that he's never run across "an epidemic affecting only young girls." When the girl dies, Preacher Dan notices two fang marks on her neck. So far, so vampiric.

But, then the picture shifts gears into a basic Western plot, with Dolores' young brother Tim (Jimmy Murphy) complaining that bad guy Buffer (Bruce Gordon) is blocking the stream up to divert water from Carter's farm. Not only that, but they gave poor Tim "a body beating" (which doesn't sound good at all). Buffer wants to force the Carters off their land and take it for himself. It's the old Rancher versus Farmer plot.

When Dr. Carter is found dead (with the tell-tale fang marks on his neck), Tim naturally thinks he was killed by the dastardly Buffer.

CURSE OF THE UNDEAD

Confronting him in the local saloon, Tim and Buffer exchange a lot of trash talk ("You're so scared, you stink out loud!") before Tim unwisely draws his gun and Buffer shoots him dead.

Dolores vows revenge, hanging posters all over town that read "Gun Wanted" and offering a hundred dollars to anyone who will kill Buffer. A dark stranger appears in town – Drake Robey (Michael Pate) and takes down the posters. Dressed all in black, Robey looks much like Richard Boone as Paladin in the TV series *Have Gun, Will Travel*, which premiered just the year before this film came out. Robey goes to the saloon and tells Buffer he's going to earn the one hundred dollars. One of Buffer's men shoots Robey at point blank range to no effect.

Preacher Dan rails against Dolores hiring a gunman when Robey appears and says he wants the job. Robey sees a thorn cross on a button worn by the preacher. Preacher Dan says it was an ordination gift; a thorn from the site of the Crucifixion.

Pate is quite wonderful as Robey. A native of Australia, Pate played many bad guys and many Native Americans in the U.S. during the 60's before going back to Australia and becoming a director. Among the films he directed was the international hit *Tim* (1979), starring a young Mel Gibson. Pate's Robey is steeped in tragedy; a lost, wandering soul yearning for rest. "The dead don't bother me – it's the living who give me trouble."

The Preacher discovers Robey's secret. Years before, when the Spanish ruled California, a man named Drago Robles murdered his own brother when he caught him with his betrothed. Consumed by grief, Drago killed himself, rose from the grave as a vampire, and killed his fiancé. In the years since, Robey has roamed the West as a gunman and a vampire, spreading death like a plague. This version of a vampire's origin – a suicide and unforgivable sin – is far more in keeping with the actual vampiric myths than the usual "victim of a vampire becomes vampire" stuff of the movies. That, and Pate's performance, gives the film a timeless, tragic quality that transcends its B-movie nature and lifts it into something almost sublime.

In the end, good and evil must square off. Preacher Dan and Drake Robey have a showdown. Robey is quite sure no bullet can harm him. He always lets the other man fire first; then he can kill him with impunity.

But Preacher Dan has an ace up his sleeve. He fires first and Robey falls, shocked that the bullet struck home and that it is destroying him. Robey falls and then crumbles to dust, leaving his clothes like a husk on the ground.

The preacher reaches into the pile of clothes and pulls out the bullet he fired. The bullet has been fashioned from Preacher Dan's thorn cross – the one that was made from the site of the Crucifixion. The most holy relic has defeated the gunman from hell.

Curse of the Undead isn't a perfect film. It's slow in spots and is filmed in the flat style of an episode of a Western TV show. Some of the acting is rather stiff. But ideas in the film, the heart of the film, is very sound. And a few scenes – Robey preying on Dolores like a lover; Robey appearing in the doorway like a dark shadow of death; Robey cringing under the shadow of a cross – achieve an almost Val Lewton style of poetry.

So, while imperfect, it is a good movie that rewards careful viewing. It is a film that actually has something to say about the struggle between good and evil. As Preacher Dan tells Dolores, "All this raving about killing and revenge is as blasphemous as praying to the devil." And Dolores replies, "If the devil can stop some of this pain in me, then I'll even pray to him."

That's one fine line and it belies the notion that the Deins wrote it as a joke. *Curse of the Undead* is worth watching. And that's no joke.

7 FACES OF DR. LAO

1964

STEVEN PEROS

Twenty-nine-year-old Charles G. Finney's first novel, *The Circus of Dr. Lao*, won the very first National Book Award for the Most Original Book of 1935. It wasn't until the early 1960's that the genius *Twilight Zone* and short story scribe, Charles Beaumont introduced it to fantasy filmmaker maestro George Pal (*The War of the Worlds*, *Tom Thumb*, *The Time Machine*), along with his own screenplay adaptation.

Finney's book — dark, adult, and cynical in tone — depicted a traveling circus that comes to a tiny, dusty Arizona town, demonstrating true magic and miracles, only to fail to impress the locals. Finney, who had traveled internationally, was satirizing his fellow Americans. The book was undoubtedly an influence on *Something Wicked This Way Comes*, whose author, Ray Bradbury, was a very vocal fan. Since that book was published while Beaumont's script adaptation of *Lao* was in development, one might theorize that Beaumont may have been similarly counter-influenced by Bradbury's book, with its ultimately un-cyni-

CINEMA BIZARRO

cal, mankind-affirming message, suitable for family consumption (unlike Finney's book). This, of course, is also a sign of director/producer George Pal's humanist guiding hand. For those who wish to learn more about the development and production of the resultant film, it is chronicled with jaw-dropping thoroughness by *Giant Beast Cinema* contributor Justin Humphreys in his Rondo Award winning, definitive biography, *George Pal: Man of Tomorrow* (beating out our own nominated book that same year).

Taking place in the fictitious Abalone, Arizona in the early 1900's (it's a Weird Western, but there are sputtering early automobiles abounding). Ed Cunningham (John Ericson), who arrived recently from the big city and runs the local newspaper, is propositioned by the mysterious and bemused Dr. Lao (who insistently pronounces his name as "low") to run a full-page ad for his circus, which will be performing for two nights. Only the audience is given a glimpse that Dr. Lao is a magical being when he lights his pipe with a flame from his own thumb in the opening images, and then waves his hand over the broken printing press, getting it to power up once again. From here on in, the locals pronounce his name so as to rhyme with "how," which is not so much an error of the filmmakers as it is a comment on the characters.

It's important to point out that, just like Marlon Brando donning "yellow face" in the 1956 film adaptation of the Pulitzer winning stage play, *Teahouse of the August Moon* (also a William Tuttle makeup), the Asian character of Dr. Lao is never the butt of the jokes. On the contrary, here (just like in the Finney novel) it is the white Americans who are being poked fun at with Lao always in the superior position. And why shouldn't he be, given that he is a magical emissary here to ultimately teach the locals a lesson about community and self-worth. Played brilliantly by Tony Randall, Lao is initially introduced as having a thick Chinese accent and spouting stereotypical "Whatsa-matta-you? You make big joke!" declarations. But the joke is on the viewer because soon after, he speaks in perfect, mellifluous English, and still later, like W.C. Fields and a carnival barker. Dr. Lao not only wants the townspeople to wonder who or what he is, but Beaumont and Pal similarly want the audience to question their own prejudices and assumptions. So, before modern audiences knee-jerkedly criticize the use of a white actor playing an Asian, do know that MGM required that a movie star be cast in the role and, at this time, there were no Asian movie stars in the US. Given this, Randall's work is sensitive, nuanced, and dignified. As a final note here, Tuttle's makeup won an Honorary Academy Award (it only became a yearly category in 1981).

It was not only Pal's idea to limit the number of magical beings at the traveling circus and retitle the film adaptation *7 Faces of Dr. Lao*, but also to have the same actor play all the circus parts, which initially made pre-*Pink Panther* Peter Sellers beg to play the role before MGM deemed him not a big enough star, preferring Randall. Now back to the story…

Cunningham has been publishing editorials against wealthy Clinton Stark (the marvelous, twice-Oscar nominated Arthur O'Connell) who is offering to buy out the entire town, purportedly as a form of philanthropy, but secretly is doing so because he alone possesses the knowledge that a railroad is coming through, which will make him turn an incalculable profit. Beaumont's depiction of Stark is rich and defies cliché. Stark is someone who had unrealistically high ideals for mankind in his youth but descended into cynical contempt with each passing disappointment in his fellow man. As noted by the circus's resident fortune teller, Apollonius of Tyana, deep down, Stark hopes to one day lose one of his bets against mankind and be shown that integrity and human spirit will endure.

As the circus opens for its two-night gig, we meet the sadly rusty and very aged Merlin (another exceptional Tuttle makeup), who is still capable of true magic, which is dismissed by the adults but understood by Mike (9-year-old Kevin Tate in a touching performance), who lost his father and lives with his widowed librarian mother, Angela (Barbara Eden). Cunningham is trying to court the young widow, but Angela insists she will love no other.

In the movie's most book-similar scene, the deluded, overbearing, town biddy, Mrs. Cassan (Lee Patrick) visits the tent of Apollonius, who, "cursed to tell the truth", informs her she will never love again, never strike oil, never grow wiser, and will die and be forgotten. It's a beautifully written and acted scene, quickly followed by Angela looking for Mike, only to wander into the tent for sideshow attraction Pan, the satyr. Pan is first portrayed by Randall but then morphs into John

CINEMA BIZARRO

Ericson, who dances around Angela, playing his lute, faster and faster, wordlessly heating up Angela into a rediscovering of her well-suppressed romantic needs. With zero dialogue, it is the power of the Leigh Harline score, Pal's filmmaking, and especially Eden's performance that sells what is inarguably the movie's most erotic scene.

On the second and final night of the circus, Dr. Lao (who confides in young Mike that he is "7,322 years old this October") projects a thinly veiled parable above the gathered crowd, exposing not only Stark's villainy but their own foolishness. When the lights come up, the key characters find themselves now sitting in the town hall, about to vote on Stark's offer. Whereas two nights earlier, they were nearly unanimously in favor, now they are unified in their refusal, a loss which Stark is proud to weather, having undergone a Scrooge-like character renaissance. But Stark's two henchmen, having gone on a drunken bender, try to destroy Dr. Lao's circus, unwittingly unleashing Lao's Loch Ness Monster (Oscar-nominated special effects by team member, Jim Danforth), before Lao and Mike contain it.

As Lao rides off the next morning, a tearful Mike juggles, a la Merlin, in tribute. Dr. Lao's earlier words to Mike echo over the soundtrack:

"Every time you watch a rainbow and feel wonder in your heart. Every time you pick up a handful of dust, and see not the dust, but a mystery, a marvel, there in your hand. Every time you stop and think, 'I'm alive, and being alive is fantastic!' Every time such a thing happens, you're part of the Circus of Dr. Lao."

Those readers who have seen *7 Faces of Dr. Lao* know full well the power of those words. I wish all who have not yet beheld the wonders of this singularly impactful fantasy film seek it out as soon as possible.

BILLY THE KID vs. DRACULA

1966

MIKE PEROS

I realize I am about to write what may be the most controversial statement in this tome, but here goes: *Billy the Kid vs. Dracula* (1966) is not as bad as they say. Don't get me wrong — it will never be confused with a good movie, and there are legitimate reasons why some vilify it. The title invites disdain, mainly because... well, Billy the Kid never met up with Dracula. In fact, the character of Billy the Kid, as written here, is so nonthreatening, the movie might as well be called "Nice Ranch Hand with a Gun vs. Dracula." But who would pay to see that? The second eponymous character (played by John Carradine) is never even referred to as Dracula; he's just your garden-variety, creepy old guy/vampire (More about his habits later).

Then, there is the William Beaudine factor. Beaudine was a journeyman director whose feature film career spanned almost fifty years. His credits include *The Ape Man* (1943), *Voodoo Man* (1944), both starring Bela Lugosi, several East Side Kids/Bowery Boys movies, including *Ghosts on the Loose* (1943, also with Lugosi), *Bowery Buck-*

aroos (1947), and the best of the Bowery Boys batch, *Blues Busters* (1950), with Sach (Huntz Hall) crooning and Slip (Leo Gorcey) scheming. Beaudine did work efficiently and quickly, earning the dubious sobriquet, "One Shot" Beaudine, and occasionally produced some decent low-budget movies. Then again, given a larger budget, he also directed two of the lesser (read "worst") Walt Disney epics, *Westward Ho, the Wagons!* (1956) and *Ten Who Dared* (1960).

Finally, John Carradine, the film's star, a veteran of over two hundred films, including classics such as *Stagecoach* (1939) and *The Grapes of Wrath* (1940), as well as the cringe-inducing *Beast of the Yellow Night* (1971) and *Blood of Ghastly Horror* (1972) has done the film no favors with his subsequent comments. When asked about his worst film, he quickly replied, *"Billy the Kid vs. Dracula"*. In another interview, Carradine said he regretted nothing — except for *Billy the Kid vs. Dracula*. This comes from a venerable actor who appeared in *Superchick* (1973), *Vampire Hookers* (1978), and *Honey Britches* (1971). Yet, *Billy the Kid...* is his only regret? Well, if you say it long enough and loud enough, people start to believe it.

As for *Billy the Kid vs Dracula*, what may prejudice a viewer begins right away, with the phoniest cinematic bat in film history punctuating the opening credits. There is also an overly emphatic theremin, which, coupled with the appearance of this wing-flapper (repeated ad-infinitum), can lead to unintended guffaws.

After a "mysterious attack" on an unfortunate victim, a somber Carradine is on a stagecoach, along with a few others, including a garrulous Mary Ann Bentley (Marjorie Bennett). At this point, Carradine's Count seems to be aimlessly moving from neck to neck, but once he sees a photo of Bentley's niece, Elizabeth (Melissa Plowman), there is no doubt as to the "neck of the woods" that Carradine is heading. After a convenient Indian massacre of the coach passengers, Carradine assumes the role of Elizabeth's uncle (it helps she's never met him)— now giving him authority to run Elizabeth's ranch.

What's astonishing is how quickly these townspeople take Carradine's identity at face value. He merely produces some "papers" and proclaims himself Mr. Underhill, Elizabeth's uncle... and that's that. Elizabeth might be looking for a father figure, but Carradine's constant leers suggest anything but paternal avuncularity. The sheriff (veteran stuntman Roy Barcroft) is also okay with the "Uncle". However, Virginia Christine's foreign maid is very concerned, since her daughter was that first victim. She also knows about vampires and has the wolfsbane to keep them at bay—too bad that Elizabeth insists that the wolfsbane be removed (This is not the first time Hollywood veterans Christine and Carradine have shared the screen. In 1959, they both appeared in *Rescue 8*, a forerunner of the 70's series *Emergency*.).

Also not taken in by Carradine's patrician demeanor is Elizabeth's beau, none other than a reformed Billy the Kid, working as her ranch hand. As played by Chuck Courtney, Billy is a sincere, albeit callow older youth, which still makes him more credible than tough-guy Robert Taylor in the 1941 *Billy the Kid*. While Billy is skeptical, he continually defers to Elizabeth's declaration of trust in her newfound uncle.

Having established himself with the all-too-trusting Elizabeth, Uncle retires, telling Elizabeth, "I am tired — I may sleep all day." Critics of this film note that Carradine's Dracula is all too visible during the daylight hours, as if this violated some holy decree. However, since these myths of Dracula's inability to exist in daylight were created by writers other than Bram Stoker, any cries of sacrilege seem fairly ridiculous. Heck, even the vampires in the *Twilight* series thrive in daylight.

As if parrying with Elizabeth and the Uncle weren't enough, Billy has to contend with Thorpe (Bing Russell), a brutal foreman who beats him up — and is in league with the Uncle. Thorpe doesn't know Uncle's true identity; he just likes Uncle for who he is. Luckily, the town Doc (a very welcome and watchable Olive Carey, widow of Western legend Harry Carey and a Western veteran herself) can both treat and commiserate with Billy. She, too, is disturbed by some strange occurrences, such as animals dying with their throats ripped open. Doc also owns a handy book on vampires, which contains such essential tidbits as "a vampire does not cast a reflection" and that "sometimes, a vampire takes a mate."

Before you can say "I do," Uncle persuades Elizabeth to bring him to the nearby cave, and is close to hypnotizing her when Billy arrives. When Billy later posits that Underhill is an impostor, the Sheriff ripostes that it "looks like that woman foreigner is getting to you." Uncle then swiftly fires Billy and locks a strangely compliant Elizabeth in her room (Elizabeth is supposed to be an adult, but no one treats her like one—a comment on the toxic masculinity of the Wild West perhaps?)

On Uncle's orders, Thorpe tries to take on Billy. However, while this Billy might be inept with his fists, he is truly Billy with his gun, shooting Thorpe and hiding the now-bitten Elizabeth at the Doc's. After Uncle demands Elizabeth's whereabouts ("Where do I find this backwoods, female pill slinger?!") he appears at the Doc's to whisk Elizabeth back to the cave—but not before the crafty Doc establishes he casts no reflection. (Uncle/Dracula is in such a hurry, he bafflingly leaves the Doc alone.) The Doc, the chastened sheriff, and Billy find the Count, and when bullets can't kill him, Billy hurls his gun, proving that while bullets have no affect, a gun can effectively knock out a vampire. Billy drives a stake through his heart, Elizabeth and Billy kiss, and the Sheriff and Doc exchange knowing smiles. Maybe there's a future for those two also…?

I don't understand why *Billy the Kid vs. Dracul*a gets no love. Carradine may just be cashing a check, but he is sinister and commanding, albeit occasionally over-the-top, while Olive Carey and Virginia Christine provide sturdy support. For a Beaudine quickie, the film has a decent pace and a few atmospheric sequences that would work better without that darn bat. Beaudine would quickly follow this with another 1966 genre mashup, *Jesse James Meets Frankenstein's Daughter*, and receive some similar critical carping. But maybe, Beaudine and his co-creators were ahead of their time—some years later, historical figures like Abraham Lincoln would take on both vampires and zombies in both novels and films. Who knew William "One Shot" Beaudine was a visionary?!

JESSE JAMES MEETS FRANKENSTEIN'S DAUGHTER

1966

TRACY MERCER

Jesse James meets Frankenstein's Daughter is a bonkers Western/Horror hybrid that, like its depiction of Mary Shelley's fictional monster, ultimately is a brain-dead, but well-meaning mess. And let's be fair, this uber low budget film was shot in only eight days, splitting its production locations between Paramount Studios and the Corriganville Movie Ranch. The film was also designed to play as a double bill with the also awesomely titled Western/Horror film mashup, *Billy the Kid vs. Dracula*, reviewed in the previous chapter.

But, before we jump into *JJMFD*'s plot, let's take a minute to discuss the pop cultural year that birthed this singular film and gives it context: 1966. One could argue 1966 represents one of the all-time coolest and innovative years for pop culture in recent memory. Gene Roddenberry's *Star Trek* took TV audiences where they had boldly not gone before and daytime TV's *Dark Shadows* saved ABC by launching Barnabas Collins

CINEMA BIZARRO

as the first Vampire with a conscience years before Anne Rice thought that could be a good idea. We also had Adam West winking his way through *Batman* in prime time, Raquel Welch taking a *Fantastic Voyage* on the silver screen, The Monkees' "Hangin' Round" launching them into the hearts of a generation and, of course, Nancy Sinatra stomping to the top of the record charts with her signature tune, "These Boots Are Made For Walkin'."

Given 1966's crucible of kitsch, it makes total sense that a low budget film would combine your father's favorite genre of the Western with a US spin on the UK Hammer Studios Dracula and Frankenstein reinterpretations to create a totally new, funky, "so bad it's good" movie. Let's talk about two fun notes concerning this magnificent title: first, this film follows the very cool tradition of movie character crossovers in horror/comedy hybrids, perhaps best-popularized by *Abbott and Costello Meet Frankenstein* in 1948 and all the sequels that followed. By 1948, the monsters were familiar and not really that scary anymore to popular filmgoing audiences, so reintroducing the beloved actors like Lugosi and Karloff and adding humor/comedy genre beats made the monsters feel fresh. Recall that by 1966, the first phase of Universal Pictures' Monster films that put Carl Laemmle's studio on the map – Bela Lugosi as *Dracula* (1931), Karloff the Uncanny in *Frankenstein* (also '31) and Claude Rains as *The Invisible Man* (1933), with their sequels – were already dusty. Pairing Universal's 1948 box office gold comedy duo, Abbott & Costello, with brand-name, old-school monsters just made good sense, and for even better films that appealed to multiple generations. *JJMFD*'s filmmakers deserve credit for leaning into a similar idea in 1966. In a way, one could also argue 1996's *Scream* pulled off the same cinematic hat trick. Afterall, the slasher craze of the 1980's had become dusty as well until along came Kevin Wiliamson's *Scream* script, that proved to be an effective slasher film (re-igniting the genre) even as it deconstructed the older horror tropes with wit and humor.

The second note about this film's title we have to point out is that it is just factually incorrect. No one actually meets Frankenstein's daughter, because this is a film about Victor Frankenstein's GRANDdaughter assuming the crazy scientist mantle in the Wild West. Talk about a high concept!

One of the beautiful things about this film is that it plays like a fever dream where logic and random plot points come and go. Follow: Our film opens sometime after 1882, which is the year the world erroneously, according to this film, believes outlaw Jesse James was gunned down by that coward, Robert Ford. In *JJMFD*, Jesse James is very much alive and up to his old murdering and robbing ways. Our film is set in America's Wild West, and we quickly learn that Victor Frankenstein's twisted granddaughter, Maria (Narda Onyx) has packed up her bags – replete with a limited number of artificially created/enhanced brains left over from her infamous relative – to move from Austria to America. Presumably, the brains have been floating in giant jars of goopy liquid since Victor Frankenstein's death and made the long, bumpy transatlantic journey intact. The film never explains these details. But we come to understand that Maria feels America is her own personal manifest destiny. Why? Well, she tells her brother and lab assistant Rudolfo (Steven Geray), they must relocate to cowboy country because it just happens to have more electrical storms than Austria. Clearly, she sees this as a huge plus for her experiments. Who wants to tell this scientist that thunderstorms and lightning occur across the globe?

What's particularly demented about this film's setup is that Maria has been kidnapping and killing immigrant children and experimenting on them. She uses her grandfather's cultivated brains on the kids with the hopes of resurrecting them to serve her as slaves. Throwing a wrench into her best efforts is none other than Rudolfo, who is secretly thwarting his sister by poisoning the doomed kids after they are successfully revived. It turns out that even in the Wild West, people notice missing children. One of those people is the beautiful Juanita (Estelita Rodriguez), whose brother has recently disappeared. She pleads with her parents Nina and Manuel not to leave town. They must find out what happened to her brother and what is happening to the town's children.

We next cut to infamous outlaw Jesse James (John Lupton) and his lunkhead servant, Hank (Cal Bolder, sporting a very 1960's Mr. Universe body) arriving in the same small town in order to join The Wild Bunch Gang. Their would-be, big-time robbery goes awry when one of the gang sells out the others to the sheriff. A deadly shootout takes the lives of the remaining gang members except for Jesse and Hank (who is wounded). When the two outlaws hide at Juanita's parents' property,

CINEMA BIZARRO

she covers for them and takes them to Dr. Frankenstein so Hank can get medical attention. From there, the plot gets more muddled as we see Maria fail to seduce Jesse, so she sends him to a pharmacy with a prescription that is actually a note announcing his real identity as an outlaw. The ruse is designed so Maria has time to experiment on Hank who she does successfully revive. Maria also learns Rudolfo has sabotaged her previous experiments and orders Hank, who she now calls Igor (!), to kill her own brother.

Meanwhile, Jesse gets caught by a sheriff deputy named Lonny (Rayford Barnes). Jesse realizes too late that it was Maria who outed his real identity and set him up. Jesse shoots and kills the deputy, returns to Maria's, only to be quickly knocked out and tied up by "Igor" who now appears to be doing Maria's bidding. Juanita, hoping to save Jesse, realizes she needs reinforcements. Juanita knows Jesse is in Maria's crosshairs so she goes with the sheriff to Maria's house, hoping Jesse can be saved by being arrested. A rowdy fight breaks out with our characters fighting for their lives. Maria orders Igor to murder Juanita, but something of old Hank must be still present as Igor turns on Maria and kills her instead. Juanita, in the chaos, manages to grab the sheriff's gun and "kills" Igor for good.

The following morning, Jesse buries his beloved Hank/Igor. It should be noted, the film makes no attempt to get closure for Juanita over her lost sibling. Her little brother isn't even an afterthought by film's end. And, as an outlaw, Jesse knows he must keep moving and there is no love connection to be had with Juanita. So, like many old school Westerns that came before and since, we fade to black on our cowboy riding off into the sunset and toward new adventures, ideally, facing relatable rival gunslingers and no further gothic horror siblings.

Also from BearManor Media

Giant Bug Cinema - A Monster Kid's Guide

Giant Beast Cinema - A Monstrous Movie Guide

H.M. Wynant - You Must Believe!

?

Made in the USA
Las Vegas, NV
05 March 2025

b85a5327-f5c9-4f94-aa2d-58cf2f4295bbR01